MTTC

English as a Second Language Practice Questions

Mometrix
TEST PREPARATION

DEAR FUTURE EXAM SUCCESS STORY

First of all, **THANK YOU** for purchasing Mometrix study materials!

Second, congratulations! You are one of the few determined test-takers who are committed to doing whatever it takes to excel on your exam. **You have come to the right place.** We developed these practice tests with one goal in mind: to deliver you the best possible approximation of the questions you will see on test day.

Standardized testing is one of the biggest obstacles on your road to success, which only increases the importance of doing well in the high-pressure, high-stakes environment of test day. Your results on this test could have a significant impact on your future, and these practice tests will give you the repetitions you need to build your familiarity and confidence with the test content and format to help you achieve your full potential on test day.

Your success is our success

We would love to hear from you! If you would like to share the story of your exam success or if you have any questions or comments in regard to our products, please contact us at **800-673-8175** or **support@mometrix.com**.

Thanks again for your business and we wish you continued success!

Sincerely,
The Mometrix Test Preparation Team

Printed in the United States of America

TABLE OF CONTENTS

Practice Test #1

1. If an educator does not know an ELL's family's language, which strategy would help him or her learn from, communicate with, and involve them in their child's education best?

a. Making use of structured interviews
b. Making use of informal conversation
c. Making use of community resources
d. Making use of oral and written histories

2. A 10th-grade English language arts (ELA) teacher has several early-advanced English learners in his class. Before reading a passage during class, students are placed into pairs to look for difficult words. They are then asked to apply different strategies to understand their meaning by using primary language cognates and morphemes. What is the reasoning for this activity?

a. Vocabulary acquisition helps support language acquisition and comprehension.
b. Skimming helps students develop test-taking skills for standardized tests.
c. Practicing cognates helps students identify which cognates are false and which are not.
d. Expanding their understanding of complex and compound sentences enhances language acquisition.

3. Which of the following statements is true regarding internal and external elements of culture?

a. Arts and literature are internal elements.
b. Traditional rituals and rites are external.
c. Nonverbal communications are internal.
d. Social roles and status are external items.

4. A middle school English Language Development (ELD) teacher notices that her students have difficulty reviewing for their social studies tests because their notes are incomplete. They explain that the teacher talks too quickly during class when they are writing notes, so they often miss some of the key words or ideas as they try to write everything down. Which strategy would best support these learners?

a. Give them all of the class notes so they don't need to worry about taking notes.
b. Teach them how to take better notes such as only writing key words, organizing based on topic, and underlining or highlighting main ideas.
c. Ask the teacher to record the lessons so they can listen to the lessons again at home.
d. Tell the teacher that she must talk much more slowly.

5. For English language learner (ELL) students who have developed grade-level English language vocabulary but are below grade level in their comprehension of spoken English syntax, how should a teacher vary the types of questions he or she asks the students aloud in class?

a. Ask questions using simple sentences.
b. Ask questions using simpler word choices.
c. Ask questions using a smaller range of words.
d. Ask questions using simpler structures and words.

6. When English language learner (ELL) students newly arrive from other countries, in which stage do their parents usually first become alarmed about their children losing their native culture and language?

a. Honeymoon stage
b. Culture shock stage
c. Integration stage
d. Acceptance stage

7. According to research findings, which statement best reflects what is true as English language learner (ELL) students shift from L1 to L2 use?

a. L1 attrition is beneficial to ELL students for their L2 acquisition.
b. L1 maintenance is important for developing L2 vocabulary.
c. L1 maintenance promotes cognitive benefits, pride, and confidence.
d. L1 attrition is not beneficial to ELLs, but (B) and (C) are correct.

8. A teacher using Specially Designed Academic Instruction in English (SDAIE) with high school English language learner (ELL) students not only teaches them subject content and English language skills but additionally gives them explicit instruction in categorizing words by their syntactic and semantic characteristics. How will this help the students develop their subject content and English language knowledge?

a. It will enable them to distinguish the main and supporting ideas better.
b. It will enable them to understand and remember English words better.
c. It will enable them to preplan and organize their compositions better.
d. It will enable them to feel less anxious and perform English tasks better.

9. A teacher with a mainstream English language classroom that includes English language learner (ELL) students as well as native English-speaking students always calls on the first student to raise a hand after he or she asks the class a question. An administrator observes the class and finds the ELL students never get to answer, although some of them do raise their hands. What instructional practice does the teacher need to change?

a. Provide enough wait time.
b. Frame questions appropriately.
c. Vary the question types by need.
d. Do all of these.

10. A teacher plans scaffolded interactions for English language learner (ELL) students by assigning them to pairs, with one partner at a higher English language proficiency (ELP) level giving peer tutoring to the other with a lower ELP level. What kind of interactions are these?

a. Student–text
b. Teacher–student
c. Student–student
d. All of these kinds

11. An English teacher for early-intermediate-level English learners from a variety of backgrounds wants his students to understand the subject–predicate pattern and subject–verb agreement for sentences. Which activity best supports this goal?

a. Comparing and contrasting sentences in English and Spanish for the English learners who speak Spanish
b. Reading English passages aloud with students so they can infer the sentence pattern from the passages
c. Explicit teaching of subject–predicate syntax through pairing students who arrange index cards, each containing a word from a meaningful sentence
d. Developing worksheets to be filled out by students individually that require students to practice subject–verb agreement

12. Which of the following describes the Self-Contained Model for teaching?

a. Emphasis on technological aids and a single teacher who provides support as issues come up.
b. Students attend typical coursework with the general population of a school and receive adaptive help from a specialist at the end of the day
c. A single teacher has students in a self-contained classroom and is responsible for both language and academic performance
d. Students are given one day out of their five-day week to spend in an ESL class while the rest of the days, they attend traditional classes.

13. In an ESL literacy rubric integrating listening, speaking, reading, and writing, which of the following belongs at an intermediate level rather than a beginning level?

a. Listening: Interpreting simple words in common, everyday situations
b. Speaking: Delivering an oral presentation about a familiar topic
c. Reading: Scanning basic or familiar texts for the important information
d. Writing: Composing simple sentences using verbs in the present tense

14. A middle school drama teacher notices that one of his English learners is shy and often has difficulty participating in class. What is an effective, student-directed Specifically Designed Academic Instruction in English (SDAIE) strategy the teacher can use after the student speaks her lines during class?

a. The teacher gives explicit feedback to the students in front of the class on pronunciation.
b. The teacher writes down strategies for making improvements.
c. The teacher coaches students on positive self-affirmations.
d. The teacher reminds students to take deep breaths and rehearse the lines.

Refer to the following for question 15:

A middle school social studies teacher has several Spanish-speaking beginning- and advanced-level English learners in his class. He pairs each of the beginning-level students with an advanced-level student to allow them to use their primary language to understand an assignment on ancient Roman history. The assignment culminates with a presentation on a famous Roman figure. However, he is worried that some of the beginner-level English learners will be too anxious to present in front of the whole class.

15. The group pairing is most likely to achieve which outcome for English learners in his class?

a. It will decrease the self-esteem of the beginning-level English language learners because they are intimidated by the level of English proficiency of the other students.
b. It will increase the assimilation of the beginning-level English learners because they are exposed to more advanced-level English speakers.
c. It will expand learners' understanding of the content because students are able to move back and forth from their first and second languages.
d. It will decrease the motivation of students to learn English because they are able to speak in their primary language.

16. ESL students are studying how to use the English language in social situations to attain the things they need and want. Which area of language covers this use?

a. Semantics
b. Pragmatics
c. Discourse
d. Lexicon

17. A kindergarten teacher has several beginning-level English learners in his class. He reads aloud the story of "Goldilocks and the Three Bears" and assesses students' comprehension of the story. Which assessment would be the MOST appropriate for his English learners?

a. Rewriting the story in their own words
b. Creating their own stories based on what they heard
c. Placing pictures of events in the story in order
d. Drawing a picture of Goldilocks and the three bears

18. When an ESL student gives an incorrect answer in class, the teacher responds by positively reinforcing the student's efforts. This is an example of which instructional process?

a. Aiding an ESL student's cognitive development
b. Minimizing the affective filter of an ESL student
c. Helping an ESL student's linguistic development
d. Instructing using multiple modalities of learning

19. Among the following English language learner (ELL) student descriptions, which one should be placed in content-based English language development (ELD) instruction rather than Specially Designed Academic Instruction in English (SDAIE)?

a. A third grader far below basic education level and at an early-intermediate ELD level
b. A seventh grader far below basic education level and at the intermediate ELD level
c. A tenth grader below the basic education level and at an intermediate level of ELD
d. All of these ELL students

20. Of the following, which is an advantage of using analytical checklists for assessment?

a. They allow for differences in assessing individual tasks across students.
b. They require additional notes to identify other notable feats observed.
c. They save time and effort by listing tasks, skills, or behaviors in advance.
d. They sometimes constrain assessment to Yes/No without quality levels.

21. In differentiating instruction for students with special educational needs, which of the following reflects the manipulation of pacing?

a. Covering the same content over twice the duration for greater reinforcement of difficult concepts
b. Covering the same content over twice the duration to investigate some concepts more thoroughly
c. Covering the same content by introducing new and unfamiliar instructional materials to address it
d. Covering the same content by enriching instruction enabling cross-curriculum student connections

22. A teacher is explaining to an ESL class that "She knew what not to do" indicates something completely different from "She knew not what to do." Into which language area does this distinction primarily fall?

a. Pragmatic
b. Academic
c. Syntactic
d. Semantic

23. When instructing ESL students with language learning disabilities, what should classroom teachers avoid?

a. Using frequent modeling
b. Slower rates of speaking
c. Multisensory instruction
d. Slang and idiomatic uses

24. A teacher arranges students to work together into diverse cooperative learning groups. What is the likely impact of this action?

a. Students will have more conflicts because they may come from competitive cultures.
b. Students will develop semantic skills.
c. It fosters a culturally inclusive classroom.
d. It creates in- versus out-group dynamics that will divide the class.

25. Students in a third-grade intermediate-level English Language Development (ELD) class are developing their classroom presentation registers. Which activity would best help them?

a. Writing out their presentations on index cards
b. Practicing pronouncing different key vocabulary words for the presentation
c. Explicit teaching and modeling of how to deliver a class presentation
d. Editing each other's work and slides for grammatical errors

26. Spanish-speaking students learning English commonly add /e/ before word-initial consonant clusters like /sp/, /st/, /spr/, /str/, and so on, for example, "espeak," "estudy," "esprinkle," "estrike." Why does this happen?

a. Their native language has no comparable such consonant clusters in it.
b. Their native language always precedes consonant clusters with the /ɛ/.
c. Their native language always separates these consonants with vowels.
d. Their native language excludes one of the consonants in each cluster.

27. Which of the following is a morphological feature?

a. The combination of roots and affixes
b. The patterns of intonation in speech
c. The pitches of a voice during speech
d. The relationship of letters to sounds

28. A teacher has a number of new English language learner (ELL) students in class at the beginning level of English language proficiency (ELP). As is normal, their receptive language skills are more developed than their expressive language skills. Which kinds of classroom assessments would be MOST appropriate to give them until they develop more ELP?

a. Textbook assessments
b. Curriculum-based assessments
c. Performance-based assessments
d. Written-response, teacher-made assessments

29. A seventh-grade social studies teacher is aware of his cultural context and understands how he was raised affects his perspectives. He understands the values of different cultures but does not necessarily agree with all of them. What is this known as?

a. Ethnocentrism
b. Ethical relativism
c. Cultural pluralism
d. Cultural relativism

30. Transactional phrases used in verbal interactions come naturally to native English speakers. For conversational support, teachers can encourage ESL students to speak English in the classroom by teaching them some of these phrases. "Let's ask the teacher about this one" is an example of such a phrase, best used for:

a. Responding to what someone says during conversation.
b. Sharing information in pair/group roleplay conversations.
c. Asking for clarification and more details in conversations.
d. Using conversation fillers while engaged in conversation.

31. Which of the following best helps validate students' cultural identities?

a. Conducting naming interviews in which students learn about the origin of their classmates' names
b. Having a show-and-tell day in which students bring something that they are interested in to class
c. Focusing on author studies and the background of authors that students have read
d. Hosting a school field trip to a local museum with information on indigenous tribes from the area

32. Two young women are at a coffee shop. They are having an animated conversation about three young men sitting at a table across the room. Much of their conversation seems cryptic, either because they do not want others to understand or because most of what they are talking about is fully present in the room, allowing them to use a verbal shorthand—or both. They don't realize a linguist is sitting at the next table, observing them and noting the relationship between orally manifested meaning (language) and contextual information conveyed through gesture, facial expression, inference, etc. In what area of linguistic study is the eavesdropper engaging?

a. Pragmatics
b. Contextual linguistics
c. Sociolinguistics
d. Etiquette orality

33. The Cognitive Academic Language Learning Approach (CALLA) and Specially Designed Academic Instruction in English (SDAIE) are examples of which of the following?

a. English for a Specific Purpose (ESP)
b. Content-based ESL models
c. Direct Instruction
d. Total Physical Response (TPR) approach

34. In a middle-school class of English language learner (ELL) students at the intermediate learning level, the teacher assigns oral reports. As each student presents a report, the teacher invites classmates to raise their hands if they need the presenter to explain or repeat anything they did not understand. How does this practice promote student communicative competence most?

a. It helps them develop social language-learning strategies.
b. It makes them more aware of grammatical components.
c. It keeps learning in the Zone of Proximal Development.
d. It applies cognitive processes to internalize language.

35. An English language learner (ELL) student whose L1 is German has a habit of writing constructions like this: "Now to the class we are going." In which of the following does the teacher need to give the student more instruction?

a. A larger English lexicon for more choice of vocabulary words
b. The differing word orders used in English versus German syntax
c. English verb tense conjugations versus German verb inflections
d. The different English versus German present progressive tense

36. When conducting informal assessments of English language learner (ELL) students at beginning English language development (ELD) levels, which of the following is a limitation of a method whereby students identify the correct picture among several to answer questions?

a. Students do not have to speak but can still communicate correct responses.
b. Students do not have opportunities to elaborate or explain their responses.
c. Students do not have to detract from performance with inadequate speech.
d. Students do not have to risk accidental wrong meanings via wrong word use.

37. Under Elementary and Secondary Education Act (ESEA), as amended by the Every Student Succeeds Act (ESSA), what must schools notify parents about regarding ESL students?

a. Their child's English proficiency level but not how this level was assessed
b. Reasons for identifying their child and need for placing in an ESL program
c. Instructional methods used in the ESL program but not educational needs
d. How they assessed English proficiency but not the child's academic status

38. To connect English language learner (ELL) parents with their children's educations, what is true about effective strategies?

a. Make sure that the parents can meet with educators during normal school hours.
b. Parents can understand collaborative, communicative school culture on their own.
c. Meeting families' basic physical, economic, and social needs is not school business.
d. Establish and maintain consistent communication with homes using parent liaisons.

39. A high school teacher wants to familiarize ELL students with standard discourse structures and conventions used in academic essays. Which activity would be most appropriate for this purpose?

a. Assign small groups to brainstorm essay topics, write short drafts, and analyze these together.
b. Give them copies of essays with key vocabulary words missing, and have them complete these.
c. Have them analyze various essay types, and identify which vocabulary and grammar they share.
d. Help them analyze provided sample essays, and make graphic organizers of various essay types.

40. A teacher has assigned English language learner (ELL) students some English-language text to read as part of a Specially Designed Academic Instruction in English (SDAIE) lesson. The teacher then asks the students to analyze and interpret the text. In what form should the teacher have them give their analyses and interpretations?

a. In written compositions only so they have a chance to organize and edit their ideas
b. In oral class discussions only to avoid writing barriers and give oral language practice
c. In both written and oral form to give equal attention to English language development (ELD) in all four of its domains
d. In individual oral exams only to avoid embarrassment in front of the rest of the class

41. For fifth-grade English language learner (ELL) students who are at the intermediate English language proficiency (ELP) level, a teacher needs to select printed instructional materials to use in a lesson about rock formation. Which of the following is the most appropriate way for the teacher to guide material selection?

a. Choosing a fifth-grade text and adapting its syntax and vocabulary
b. Substituting manipulatives and graphics for printed text materials
c. Substituting a concise outline of key subject facts instead of texts
d. Choosing a fourth- or third-grade text to match student ELP levels

42. A teacher presents a lesson in which students in her English Language Development (ELD) class have paired up to come up with rhyming words such as "car," "bar," and "far." She focuses on phonemes from the English language that may not be common in other languages such as the /schwa/, /th/, and /r/. Each pair is given a word that they must find rhymes for and present to the class. What domain of language is she developing in her students?

a. Phonology
b. Syntax
c. Phonetics
d. Morphology

43. A teacher has a number of English language learner (ELL) students within a mainstream English language classroom. These students are at intermediate (mainstreamed at parental request), early-advanced, and advanced levels of English language proficiency (ELP). Which of the following strategies could the teacher most easily use to support their learning?

a. Technologies
b. Peer tutoring
c. Team teaching
d. Paraprofessionals

44. A new ESL student's parents speak no English. They are intimidated by both the language barrier and the differences between the new American school and the schools in their native country. The ESL teacher contacts a local community center, which not only provides an interpreter, but also helps the teacher explain American cultural customs and school practices to the parents. The parents are then receptive to the teacher's invitation to join in school activities and share their culture with other students and families. In what way(s) has the teacher advocated for the new ESL student?

a. Facilitating parental involvement in their ESL child's education
b. The teacher has advocated for the student in all of these ways
c. Communicating and collaborating with parents of ESL students
d. Accessing community resources to enhance the ESL education

45. ESL student Lana says, "*Hide, hid, hidden* is different from *walk, walked* or *like, liked;* but it is the same as "*bite, bit, bitten.*" Which cognitive process is she using here to learn English-language rules?

a. Memorization
b. Categorization
c. Generalization
d. Metacognition

46. Among the following choices, which is MOST advisable for providing a culturally inclusive learning environment in schools?

a. Assigning homogeneous group learning activities so students with similar backgrounds interact
b. Assigning independent learning activities to prevent cultural conflicts during student interaction
c. Assigning cooperative group learning activities for students of different backgrounds to interact
d. Assigning students to fixed pairs so every partner gets exposure to a different background

47. Which of the following examples describes a summative assessment?

a. A lab report completed as a homework assignment
b. A weekly vocabulary quiz on science content words
c. A teacher's observations of a student as he completes a science experiment
d. A science test given at the end of a unit on adaptations

48. A teacher, observing a new English language learner (ELL) student's aversion to making an oral presentation before the class, is trying to determine whether this is caused by a lack of confidence with the English language or lack of personal self-confidence. When she consults with a colleague whether to get the student coaching in EL speaking skills or individual counseling, the colleague suggests the student's attitude could be due to cultural values instead. Investigating, the teacher confirms this. Which factor MOST influenced the teacher's initial attribution of the student's attitude to linguistic or personal rather than cultural causes?

a. The teacher's ignorance about the student's home culture
b. The teacher's own cultural values, beliefs, and assumptions
c. The teacher's own history of lacking confidence in childhood
d. The teacher's lack of familiarity with the student as a person

49. English language learner (ELL) Jose's teacher helps him build his English vocabulary by pointing out and listing Spanish–English cognates, showing him their identical or similar spelling and modeling and explaining their differences in pronunciation. What is this instructional strategy mostly an example of?

a. Using the student's prior L1 knowledge
b. Teaching students decoding skills
c. Systematic instruction in phonics
d. Applying word analysis methods

50. In screening and assessment instruments, what is an example of test sensitivity?

a. How often a test over-identifies or under-identifies target problems
b. How much potential a test has to offend or harm the test-taker
c. How often a test accurately rules out a problem it is meant to test
d. How often a test accurately identifies a problem it is meant to test

51. A second-grade English Language Development (ELD) teacher invites parents to participate in an after-school event. She notices that communication with the family is only with the mother and never the father. She even called home, and when she spoke with the father, he said that she should speak with Amal's mother. Which of the following may be the best explanation for why this occurs?

a. In Amal's culture, the mother usually deals with children's education.
b. Amal's father does not care about his schooling.
c. Culturally, parents are uninvolved in school because they defer to the teacher.
d. Amal's father does not speak English well enough to talk about school.

52. A teacher has decided to incorporate Total Physical Response strategies into her classroom instruction. She will:

a. Break from academic instruction every hour for 10 minutes of organized exercise.
b. Involve her students in a series of physical activities in response to her instructions and requests.
c. Break for academic instruction every hour for five minutes of independent exercise.
d. Break from academic instruction two times a day (excluding lunch) for guided meditation practice and Brilliant Mind exercises.

53. A classroom teacher with several mainstreamed ESL students is frustrated. She has noted that few of their parents come to parent-teacher conferences, and those who do, come inconsistently and have little to say. She is aware that many of them have limited English skills and also that several have very young children at home. What can she do to encourage the parents to increase their participation in their children's education?

a. Drop in unexpectedly at their homes with a gift of freshly baked bread or cookies.
b. Send home an announcement about a Foreign Parents' night, in which foods from many lands will be featured and for which they will be the featured speakers.
c. Invite several parents from the same or similar cultures to work with their children and a translator if one is available, and create a classroom presentation on some cultural aspect that will be of interest to the students. For example, Mexican and other Central American parents might present a slideshow on the Day of the Dead, followed by a show-and-tell of objects used in that celebration.
d. Nothing. They have made it clear to her that they have priorities that do not include the needs of her student, their child. It's best if she simply expects less of them and takes it upon herself to provide additional academic and emotional support to the poor child, who is clearly being neglected.

54. An elementary school is preparing for parent–teacher conferences. Which of the following is NOT necessarily a consideration that the school and teachers should make with families of English learners?

a. Having appropriate interpretation services available
b. Being flexible for meeting times because some families work
c. Considering alternatives to in-person conferences
d. Providing refreshments for parents, so they feel welcome

55. A 10th-grade math teacher has an early-intermediate English language learner in her class. She administers a math assessment on a unit on triangles that is predominantly comprised of word problems. What kind of test accommodations should she offer the student to address his needs while still assessing his abilities?

a. Give the student an open book test, so he or she can look up formulas he or she doesn't know.
b. Allow the student to ask questions during the test.
c. Reduce the number of words in the word problems so that the student only does the calculation portions.
d. Offer the student extended time to complete the exam.

56. Many students in the United States are bilingual. Some of them are simultaneously bilingual, whereas others are sequentially bilingual. Which statement best describes the difference between these two?

a. Simultaneous bilingualism is when both English and the primary language are used in the classroom, whereas sequential bilingualism is when the languages alternate, whether by days, classes, or weeks.
b. A student who has two home languages is simultaneously bilingual, whereas a student who has one home language other than English is known as sequentially bilingual.
c. Simultaneous bilingualism means that students are able to use both languages interchangeably, whereas sequential bilingualism means that students are only able to use them in different contexts.
d. Simultaneous bilingualism is when the primary and secondary language are learned at the same time, whereas sequential bilingualism is when one language is learned after the other.

57. English language learner (ELL) students may, like young children developing native English, apply a rule for regular verb conjugation to irregular verbs as well, for example, "goed" instead of "went" or "freezed" instead of "froze." What is the term for the process that these errors demonstrate?

a. Memorization
b. Categorization
c. Generalization
d. Overgeneralization

58. Which of these reflects a teaching practice that helps establish an inclusive learning environment?

a. Ensuring consistency and equity by using a single teaching method with all students
b. Varying learning activities, assignments, and teaching strategies for different needs
c. Focusing on cultural diversity by devoting a special class to the study of this subject
d. Providing students with a sense of safety through not setting rules to restrict them

59. Of the following, which is an effective strategy for intercultural interactions?

a. Basing ideas about people's overall competence on a specific competence area
b. Being honest about discomfort interacting with people from other cultures
c. Being receptive to new or unexpected information about a culture or cultural group
d. Being considerate not to embarrass others by overtly explaining cultural mores

60. Which of the following is a primary reason to include a rubric when assigning a project or paper to students?

a. To protect the educator from accusations of unfair grading
b. To be able to reuse assignments between classes
c. To ensure students are evaluated consistently
d. To allow the teacher to easily compare student performance

61. A student is enrolled in an American school, having just arrived from another country days before. He never heard English in his isolated home village and was never exposed to it via TV, radio, the Internet, nor in any other fashion. His native language differs radically from English. An educational specialist who speaks his language gives him a battery of tests in his L1 and reports his IQ and other scores are intellectually and adaptively in the top 1% of the population. In addition to English language learner (ELL) instruction, which referral is most indicated?

a. Student study team (SST)
b. Gifted and talented education (GATE)
c. Special education
d. Intervention programs

62. A class of all English language learner (ELL) students includes two students with intellectual disabilities and three students with specific learning disabilities. Their teacher differentiates instruction to accommodate the ______ needs of these students.

a. academic
b. linguistic
c. cognitive
d. cultural

63. In differentiating instruction of a multidisciplinary thematic unit for ninth-grade English language learner (ELL) students, which of the following applies?

a. ELLs should be grouped only homogeneously to encourage their team-using behaviors.
b. ELLs should be grouped only heterogeneously to encourage all students to participate.
c. Teachers should read aloud portions of the texts they use in the unit to the entire class.
d. Teachers should prevent or discourage the use of sticky notes and highlighting in text.

64. A high school science teacher has a group of beginning-intermediate-level English learners in her class. She has students answer questions regarding the parts of a cell and share them with the class. Which is the best way of lowering students' affective filters in her class?

a. Collecting all written work and correcting every mistake that students make regarding grammar, spelling, and punctuation
b. Having students work together in small groups to share their answers
c. Calling students randomly to give answers so that she knows every student is engaged
d. Not choosing any of the English language learners to give answers so they don't have to speak in front of the class

65. What is the BSM, and what is it designed to establish?

a. The Bilingual Strategies Method establishes effective instructional methods for mainstreamed bilingual students.
b. The Bilingual Syntax Measure is a tool designed to assess oral language proficiency and dominance between two languages.
c. The Burke-Stanley Milestone establishes points along the continuum from little English to full fluency.
d. The Babcock Statistical Model establishes a measurable baseline for bilingual educators.

66. Recent research from 2014 finds that, when teachers give English language learner (ELL) students electronic instead of handwritten feedback on their written compositions

a. the feedback was less explicit and systematic.
b. the feedback resulted in far superior revision.
c. the feedback did not address student needs.
d. the feedback gave equivalent effectiveness.

Refer to the following for question 67:

An advanced placement physics teacher has several advanced-level English learners in her class. She is required to use a textbook assigned by the district based on what has been formally adopted by their state department of education. She gives a variety of tests including those that are provided by the textbook publisher.

67. What is the main benefit of using this test type as opposed to other types of exams?

a. It allows students to demonstrate their knowledge through a variety of means including using several different pieces of work by the students.
b. It is easier to grade, and the teacher does not have to spend time writing another examination.
c. It allows for authentic assessment of knowledge because students will have a chance to incorporate their own opinions.
d. It aligns closely with the state standards and the content knowledge required for the advanced placement exam.

68. A high school teacher notices that an English learner in his class is able to speak English with her peers during lunch and breaks; however, she has difficulty speaking English in his chemistry class. Which description offers the best explanation for this difference?

a. The student lacks syntactic knowledge used in chemistry.
b. The student is shy and doesn't like talking during class.
c. The student has acquired BICS but not CALP English language skills.
d. The student doesn't have a strong grasp of the pragmatic features of the English language.

69. A middle school English teacher is planning a lesson incorporating Specially Designed Academic Instruction in English (SDAIE) for a group of early-advanced English learners. Which of the following would be most appropriate and effective to use with students at this proficiency level to promote their English language development in reading?

a. Simplifying passages being used so that when students read, they are able to comprehend the text and answer questions
b. Choosing and displaying language development objectives for the reading lesson
c. Avoiding texts with figurative language and idioms to support student understanding
d. Giving students organizers with blanks to fill in as they read to help them understand the passage

70. Which of the following are included as guidelines for innovating and revising school curriculum to be multicultural?

a. Countries and cultures of origin
b. Not histories of oppression
c. Implementers but not autobiography
d. Local responses, not global inclusions

71. A school district has eight elementary schools; all schools have large ESL student populations, and the ESL students come from more than twenty different nations, all speaking different languages. For this district, which ESL program model would be most suitable?

a. The early-exit bilingual program model
b. The late-exit bilingual program model
c. The model of pull-out classes for ESLs
d. The sheltered English program model

72. In order to develop CALP, which of the following methods is most likely to succeed?

a. Give students a variety of communication experiences. Informal conversation with a peer, formal presentation before a class, personal journal writing, and reports will all contribute to the development of a student's CALP.
b. Group students homogeneously so that they can work on projects with a variety of different individuals and learn flexibility in learning styles.
c. Building literacy skills in all content areas will improve CALP and increase language and abstract thinking skills across the board.
d. No methods will work; CALP is a subconscious, natural process that develops in its own time and at its own speed. Attempting to streamline the process is likely to backfire, producing a speaker who is hesitant and insecure.

73. When assessing English language learner (ELL) students in their L1s, which of the following is the MOST valid consideration?

a. Standardized assessment instruments are equally easy to obtain in the L1s.
b. Qualified practitioners to assess ELLs in their L1s are as available as in the L2.
c. Students assessed in their L1s can be overidentified with disorders or delays.
d. Students assessed in their L1s can be under-identified for disorders or delays.

74. A teacher has a new English language learner (ELL) student in her class at the beginning of the school year. The student understands and speaks some English, but this is his first American school enrollment, and there are no relevant previous school records. What is the first thing the teacher should do?

a. Assess the student's language proficiency level.
b. Assess the student's previous knowledge in L1.
c. Give the student scaffolding for language tasks.
d. Monitor the student's English language progress.

75. An eighth-grade English Language Development (ELD) teacher is working on independent and dependent clauses with her students. Which activity would be the best first step to help her English language learners understand these two types of clauses?

a. Give examples of both dependent and independent clauses, and have students in groups infer the differences between the two.
b. Have students watch a video about sentence types and come up with examples.
c. Give a list of prepositional phrases and coordinating conjunctions to understand dependent and independent clauses.
d. Introduce subjects and predicates with sentence strips to teach the concept of clauses.

76. A ninth-grade world history teacher front-loads vocabulary from her unit on ancient Greece with a group of advanced-level English language learners. What effect will this have on her students?

a. Enable better comprehension of concepts that students may not know
b. Support diverse learning styles to increase language learning
c. Help build interpersonal language skills for when they will have group work
d. Reduce their schemata to help promote confidence and minimize anxiety

77. Which of the following classroom practices is LEAST effective with regard to second language acquisition:

a. Presenting sufficient and meaningful reading and writing experiences for students to practice strategies
b. Keeping all reading and writing activities at the student's current reading level
c. Reviewing and re-teaching as required to ensure that students have integrated essential content
d. Daily introduction of a few new words or concepts

78. According to the NCLB Act (2001), federal funds under Title III can be used:

a. To supplement federal, state, or local public funds for ESL programs.
b. As the main budget for funding federal, state, or local ESL programs.
c. For the Full-Time Equivalent (FTE) hiring of teachers for ESL programs.
d. To administer ESL programs that have no other sources for funding.

79. A third-grade teacher notices that one of her English learners tends to withdraw when she touches his shoulder. What is important for her to consider when she discusses this with his school counselor?

a. There may be physical abuse at home.
b. He may not like her much so doesn't want to be near her.
c. Some cultures do not have high levels of physical contact.
d. He may be scared of her as an authority figure.

80. What 1982 Supreme Court case established the right to a free education for undocumented immigrant children?

a. Plyler v. Doe
b. Lau v. Nichols
c. Meyer v. Nebraska
d. Castaneda v. Pickard

81. Which of the following is a primary tenet of a balanced reading program?

a. Combining a range of activities that address phonics, fluency, and comprehension
b. Using students' own stories to develop literacy
c. Focusing on vocabulary development to improve reading comprehension
d. Developing fluency as a means to build literacy

82. Which of the following scaffolding strategies or approaches for developing English language learners' (ELLs') cross-curricular English language reading and writing proficiency are typically most visual and nonlinguistic in nature?

a. Learning logs
b. Shared reading
c. Graphic organizers
d. Interactive journals

83. A third-grade teacher is seeking to foster a culturally supportive classroom. Which of the following best describes a strategy she can use to do this?

a. Fostering high standards by using Tier 3 academic language throughout her classes
b. Encouraging language development through English-only methods and practices
c. Providing simplified versions of activities for English learners to be successful
d. Maintaining high expectations by giving enough wait time for responses and smiling

84. A teacher promotes autonomy in English language learner (ELL) students through debriefing. Which is correct about this strategy?

a. Debriefing always involves reflection.
b. Reflection always involves debriefing.
c. Debriefing always uses text features.
d. Debriefing is equal to self-evaluation.

85. An English language learner (ELL) student from Japan is in a class where the current assignment involves competing with classmates to see who can achieve the highest score in an academic game or contest. Instead of using her high intelligence and competence to defeat classmates, however, she uses it to help them succeed. What is the most likely cultural reason for her behavior?

a. The ELL student, intimidated by being new to the country and school, wants to please peers.
b. The ELL student, being new in the country, school, and class, is trying to make new friends.
c. The ELL student was raised in a culture valuing group cooperation over individual competition.
d. The ELL student feels inferior to classmates due to language barriers and is afraid to compete.

86. At an elementary school, faculty members in the school ESL program support the participation of students' families in school projects and other activities. They also consistently engage student families in making decisions about school programs. Awareness of which factors that influence language development is most demonstrated by these educator practices?

a. As children's first teachers, family can teach better if they know more about language instruction.
b. When families have positive attitudes toward school, their children are more likely to develop ELP.
c. Engagement in school activities helps family model purposeful English communication for children.
d. Family members can better evaluate language instruction effectiveness with curricular familiarity.

87. Which of the following characteristics accurately describes authentic assessment techniques?

a. They are norm-referenced
b. They are designed to build higher-order thinking skills
c. They allow students to choose from a set of teacher-prepared responses
d. They measure students' performance at a specific point in time

88. A fourth-grade teacher has a new English learner who has recently immigrated to the United States and enrolled in her class halfway through the school year. She notices that this student seems eager to participate and share about her culture. Which stage is this student most likely experiencing in the acculturation process?

a. Euphoria
b. Cultural fatigue
c. Adjustment
d. Culture shock

89. According to Stephen Krashen's theory of second-language acquisition, which method is best?

a. Letting students produce the L2 when they are ready
b. Forcing early student production of the new language
c. Correcting student production in the second language
d. Extensive drilling and consciously using grammar rules

90. An elementary school has adopted a policy to promote cultural diversity. Which steps could the school take to best promote this goal?

a. Invite parents and community members into the classroom to tell about their careers.
b. Put up posters on the walls that show many different cultures, and include languages on the posters that students speak as their home language.
c. Have monthly multicultural events like talent shows.
d. Train teachers in multicultural diversity, and revise the curriculum to be inclusive of cultures.

91. An English language learner (ELL) student writes this sentence: "Understanding spoken English and speaking in English is harder for me than reading and writing English." What is the error in this sentence?

a. The word order
b. The tense of the verb
c. Subject–verb agreement
d. None of these

92. An English language learner (ELL) student has learned the *-ed* ending rule for past tense and past perfect tense with regular English verbs, for example, *look, looked, have* or *had looked* or *stay, stayed,* or *have* or *had stayed,* and so on. Now, additionally, she determines that certain irregular English verbs share common vowel changes, for example, *speak, spoke, spoken; freeze, froze, frozen; awake, awoke, awoken,* and so on. In which cognitive process is the student engaging by observing and differentiating these two rules?

a. Memorization
b. Generalization
c. Categorization
d. Overgeneralization

93. Which of the following is the best example of a teacher question during a Specially Designed Academic Instruction in English (SDAIE) chemistry lesson to promote critical thinking skills?

a. What are the names of all seven of the noble gases?
b. Of the gases we discussed, which ones are noble?
c. Which of the gases we discussed are inert gases?
d. Is it easy or hard to compound noble gases? Why?

94. Regarding how teachers can engage parents of English language learner (ELL) students when the parents lack English language skills and the teacher does not speak their language, which of these is true?

a. The teacher learning some common words and phrases in their language will do no good.
b. The teacher should use the student to translate rather than look for a bilingual interpreter.
c. The teacher giving contacts of bilingual staff seems like passing the parents off to others.
d. The teacher can inform parents of adult literacy learning opportunities in their community.

95. Which of the following is NOT considered a dialectal difference?

a. Hindi and Urdu
b. Beijing and Hong Kong Chinese
c. New York City and Los Angeles dialects
d. African American Vernacular English and Southern United States English

96. An English language learner (ELL) student has just learned the English word *focus*. Without further instruction, she is able to say, "This week we focus on the Civil War in American history. Last month we focused on the Revolutionary War in American history, but we are not focusing on that now." She has used ______ memory to generate the forms new to her.

a. procedural
b. declarative
c. semantic
d. episodic

97. What impact did the No Child Left Behind Act of 2001 have on school funding and English learners?

a. Schools must measure and share student results, including those of English learners, on state standardized tests to receive federal funds.
b. Schools should not include English learners in their school results for state standardized tests to receive funding.
c. All classes must have English learners to receive federal funding so that they are integrated into mainstream classes.
d. Schools must offer all state standardized tests to English learners in the language of their choice and report that to the state.

98. What is an important consideration when selecting diverse literature?

a. Is the author well-known to the students?
b. Does the book present stereotypical depictions of diverse characters?
c. Does the book include several different languages for students to read in?
d. Is the author still alive today and available for a talk at the school?

99. Which statement is characteristic of behavioral theories of language acquisition?

a. Classroom methodology should incorporate repetition and reward.
b. Cooperative grouping is essential to learning because humans are social creatures.
c. Language learners use interlanguage before they fully begin to use their second language.
d. Comprehensible input that is slightly higher than the student's level is key to learning.

100. Students in a second-grade beginning level English Language Development (ELD) class are practicing minimal pairs that differ by one phoneme such as "sap" and "tap." How does practicing in this way help promote English learners' phonemic awareness?

a. By enhancing their ability to distinguish different phonemes
b. By promoting their connected speech abilities
c. By supporting communicative competence
d. By differentiating rhymes that students need to learn

Answer Key and Explanations for Test #1

1. C: If the educator does not know the English language learner's family's language, he or she will not be able to conduct structured interviews with them in their language or have informal conversations with them in their language. He or she will also not be able to listen to or read written histories from the family in their language. The educator's best choice of strategy would be to make use of community resources to find other people who know the family's language and are willing to serve as interpreters and translators between the family and educator.

2. A: Applying strategies to try to understand difficult vocabulary words not only allows learners to develop their English language skills but also improves comprehension. Both considering cognates and morphemes are skills that strong readers use to understand passages. Although an outcome of practicing these skills may be improved test taking skills, that should not be the primary reason for this activity. Moreover, using cognates should not be for simply trying to determine which words are true and false cognates but to aid comprehension.

3. C: Nonverbal communication patterns are examples of internal elements of culture. Arts and literature are external, not internal elements (A) of culture. Traditional rituals and rites are internal, not external (B) elements of culture. Social roles and status are internal, not external (D) elements of culture. Other internal cultural elements include customs, beliefs, values, mores, expectations, family structures, gender roles, and work and leisure patterns. Other external cultural elements include government, religious structures, language, technology, food, shelter, and clothing.

4. B: Although offering notes can support students in the immediate situation, the best long-term solution is to help students learn how to take notes. Research has shown that strong note-taking skills promote academic achievement. Asking the teacher to slow down is an important accommodation, but even if the teacher does slow down, English learners must still know how to identify key words and ideas being shared by any teacher. Recording the lesson may provide a short-term solution, but it will require an extensive amount of time for the learner, and it is possible that the students may not have access to technology that would allow them to listen to the recording.

5. A: The teacher should use simple sentence structures for these students instead of compound, complex, or compound-complex sentence structures. The teacher need not use simpler word choices (B) because these students have developed English language vocabulary at grade-level difficulty. Neither does the teacher need to use a smaller range of words (C) for the same reason; the students know an equal number of grade-level vocabulary words as native English-speaking classmates. The teacher needs only to vary the sentence structure of questions but not the choice of words in them (D).

6. C: In the honeymoon (A) or euphoric stage, English language learner (ELL) students are excited to learn about their new environment. In the culture shock stage (B), they become overwhelmed as they begin to realize all the cultural differences and have difficulty coping with surroundings and linguistic and social signals they cannot comprehend. In the integration stage (C), ELL students begin integrating new cultural elements. Some replace old values with new ones; others find ways to maintain both in peaceful coexistence. This is the stage wherein many immigrant parents first become alarmed about their children losing their original values and traditions. In the acceptance (D) stage, ELLs accept and may combine both cultures and can interact comfortably in mainstream culture. In this stage, many immigrant parents try to prevent their children from adopting mainstream culture for fear they will reject or forget their native cultures, which often happens.

7. D: Research finds that losing their L1s does not benefit English language learner (ELL) students in acquiring the L2 (A). To the contrary, studies show that maintaining the L1 is important to aid ELL students for developing their vocabularies in the L2 (B), for the cognitive benefits they derive from bilingualism, and for the pride and self-confidence (C) they derive from retaining their original languages as they acquire a new one.

8. B: The teaching practice described will help English language learner (ELL) students with comprehension and memory for new English words by giving them a learning strategy of categorizing words by their characteristics of structure and meaning. The teacher has taught them a cognitive tool they can use in various academic contexts and independently build their subject content and English language proficiency (ELP). Syntactic and semantic word classification is unrelated to differentiating main and supporting ideas (A) in reading or writing (or listening or speaking). Grouping words in categories will not help the students plan or organize compositions (C); it will only help them remember and retrieve the most appropriate words for compositions. While reducing performance anxiety with English tasks (D) may be a by-product of improved English word comprehension and retention, it is not the main purpose or a direct result of this learning strategy; the comprehension and retention are.

9. A: By calling on the first student to raise a hand, the teacher is not providing enough wait time for English language learner (ELL) students, who often need longer times than native English-speaking students to process the question content, potentially translate it into their L1s and formulate responses in their L1s, and then translate those responses into English before they are ready to raise their hands. All ELLs except those who have attained native-like English language proficiency (ELP) levels typically undergo this process. The question does not provide information to know whether the teacher frames his or her questions appropriately (B) or varies the types of questions he or she asks according to different student language needs (C); he or she may or not do these things. Hence, it is impossible to say whether the teacher needs to do these (D) or already does them.

10. C: Based on the description, these are primarily student–student interactions as they involve peer tutoring. While the tutoring could involve reading a text (A), the description does not say this; they could just as well be tutoring peers in English listening or speaking skills or practicing English writing skills. The teacher's only role described here was assigning the students to pairs. If the pairs then work independently with minimal teacher guidance, it is not primarily a teacher–student (B) interaction. Because (C) is correct, (D) is incorrect.

11. C: Although students can acquire a language without explicit teaching of syntax, systematic and explicit teaching of syntax structures can expedite learning. Although comparing sentence structures from different languages is useful, it is important to consider the language background of learners. If all learners do not speak Spanish, it should not be the only method of teaching subject–predicate pattern and agreement. Worksheets can be helpful but should be used in moderation and come after explicit and direct teaching.

12. C: Self-Contained Model. The One Teacher Approach is one in which a single teacher working in a self-contained classroom carries the responsibility for her students' linguistic and academic achievement. This allows for integration of language skills on a progressive scale while learning academic English.

13. B: Delivering an oral presentation on a familiar topic is an example of an intermediate-level speaking activity in an ESL literacy rubric that integrates listening, speaking, reading, and writing. The other options are examples of beginning-level activities for listening, reading, and writing in an integrated ESL literacy rubric. Examples of intermediate-level activities include listening for the main ideas and most of the supporting details in factual/expository material about everyday topics; reading and analyzing authentic prose material about topics familiar to the student; and being able to write compositions with two or more paragraphs, including a topic sentence and supporting details.

14. C: It is important to help students develop skills before, during, and after speaking activities. One strategy is to have students engage in positive self-affirmations after speaking. Taking deep breaths and rehearsing is also a good strategy; however, it should occur before speaking. Answer A is not helpful because it can embarrass the student to give feedback in front of the class. Answer B is teacher directed rather than student directed.

15. C: Using the primary language to support learning has been shown to increase not only content learning but also learning of the English language. Advanced students can explain concepts in the primary language to beginning-level students, ensuring that they continue to grow in the content areas as they learn English. Assimilation is the erasure of a student's home culture, so allowing for home language in the classroom would not promote assimilation.

16. B: Pragmatics is the study of how language is used socially to meet one's needs and wants. Semantics (A) is the study of how words, phrases, clauses and sentences express meanings. Discourse (C) is the conventions of a language that express historical and cultural meanings; or language used to implement intellectual and social community life; or a formal, extended linguistic expression of ideas. Lexicon (D) is vocabulary, either generally or of a specific subject.

17. C: In kindergarten, English learners may or may not have writing skills, so assessing them through rewriting the story would be inappropriate both for the grade level and the language level of students. Although drawing a picture of a character may seem appropriate, to assess their comprehension, students should be tasked with placing events in the story in order. This can be done through ordering pictures of events in the story or can be done by asking students to draw the main events in a story.

18. B: By providing positive reinforcement, the teacher's response helps the ESL student feel his/her efforts are appreciated. This maximizes student self-esteem and motivation and minimizes student anxiety. ESL students experiencing high anxiety and/or low motivation or self-esteem tend to block instructional input with the "wall" of the affective filter (cf. Krashen). The teacher's response is not targeting cognitive development (A) or linguistic development (C), or addressing different learning styles via multiple learning modalities (D); it is targeting the affective filter by lowering it.

19. A: The third grader whose English language development (ELD) level is early intermediate should be placed in content-based ELD because of the student's lower grade level, lower English language proficiency (ELP), more time to learn academic content, and need to improve ELP now before academic content becomes more difficult. The seventh grader (B) and tenth grader (C) should be placed in Specially Designed Academic Instruction in English (SDAIE) because of their higher grade levels, intermediate levels of ELP, and below or far below basic educational levels relative to their grade levels to receive more instruction in academic content areas as they have comparatively less time to learn this content. Therefore, option D is incorrect.

20. C: Using analytical checklists as assessment tools has the advantage of saving time and effort by listing the tasks, skills, or behaviors to be performed and assessed in advance. They also have the advantage of making assessment uniform across students relative to tasks and/or their components, making choice A incorrect. They do require additional notes for teachers to identify other notable feats that teachers observe students accomplishing beyond the designated tasks (B), but this is a disadvantage. Although some checklists include performance levels similarly to rubrics, others constrain assessment to Yes/No responses (D), another disadvantage.

21. A: Four dimensions along which curriculum and instruction can be modified, for both challenged and advanced students, are pacing, depth, complexity, and novelty. Taking twice as long to cover the same content while additionally reinforcing difficult concepts reflects differentiating instruction through pacing. Taking twice as long to cover the same content while investigating some concepts more thoroughly (B) reflects differentiation through depth. Covering the same content by introducing new and unfamiliar materials (C) reflects differentiation through novelty. Covering the same content by enriching instruction and enabling students to make connections across the curriculum (D) not usually expected at their grade levels reflects differentiation through complexity.

22. C: This distinction is primarily syntactic because the word order in each sentence is different, changing the meaning of each. While meaning is affected, the distinction is not primarily semantic because semantics is primarily related to the meanings of words, phrases, and clauses/sentences themselves rather than to how their meanings are affected by word order and sentence structure. It is not pragmatic, which refers to how we use language socially to get what we need or want. It is not academic (i.e., related to formal subjects of study in school).

23. D: Experts advise classroom teachers to avoid using slang and idiomatic expressions when teaching ELLs with language learning disabilities. Though these students will eventually need to understand some idioms, teachers should not employ them initially with ESL students having concomitant language LDs. Experts do advise classroom teachers to model frequently (A) for these students, to speak more slowly (B), and to use multisensory/multimodal teaching methods (C).

24. C: Cooperative learning groups foster higher levels of interaction among students, which provides a classroom that supports diverse learning environments and is inclusive. Although conflicts may occur, with proper support, students will be able to overcome issues and work together. Semantic skills deal with understanding the meaning of language. Cooperative groups do not necessarily enhance semantic skills, although it might support better communication skills. Finally, it won't necessarily divide the class unless competition among groups is a prominent part of the class structure.

25. C: Language registers are different tones, vocabulary, sentence structures, and even volume used in different situations. Consider how speaking during a presentation differs from working in small groups in a classroom. The classroom presentation register often includes things like a strong voice that can be heard by the entire class and a varied tone that keeps the audience's interest. Although being able to pronounce words is important, that has to do with phonology rather than discourse.

26. B: Unlike English, Spanish always precedes these consonant clusters with /e/, for example, *esperar* (to hope or await), *estudiar* (to study), *espresso, estrella* (star). The students are transferring this feature to English words with word-initial consonant clusters. These consonants do exist in their native language (A). Their native language does include these consonants in clusters, not separated by vowels (C). None of the consonants in these clusters is excluded from their native language (D).

27. A: How word roots and affixes (i.e., prefixes, infixes, and suffixes) are combined to create words in a language is a feature of morphology. Intonation patterns in speech (B), vocal pitch when speaking (C), and letter–sound relationships (D) or phonics are all phonological features.

28. C: English language learner (ELL) students at the beginning level of English language proficiency (ELP) will understand more of what they hear and read in English (receptive) than what they can say or write in English (expressive). Thus, textbook assignments (A) will be difficult for the, as these often will require them to write their responses in English, like teacher-made tests requiring written responses (D) will. Curriculum-based assessments (B) may or may not require spoken or written responses. However, performance-based assessments (C) will allow ELLs to demonstrate what they know and can do without having higher levels of proficiency in speaking and writing English.

29. D: Cultural relativism is the idea that all thoughts, words, and actions exist in a cultural context. On the other hand, ethnocentrism is the idea that one's culture and cultural values are the norm. In this perspective, individuals are unable to understand other cultural values and beliefs. Ethical relativism is similar, but it is the belief that morals and values are all formed in accordance with societal, cultural, and individual perspectives and experiences. Cultural pluralism is the idea that there are many different cultures within a society or country.

30. B: The phrase given is an example of one best used for sharing information and role-play activities during paired and group work in the classroom. Examples of phrases for responding to someone during conversations (A) include "Really? That's interesting"; "That's great/That's terrible" or "I guess so/I guess not." Examples of phrases asking for clarification and more details (C) include "What do you mean?"; "Really? Why?"; "What about...?"; or "So then what happened?". Examples of conversation fillers (D) include "Well,..."; "You know,..."; "You see,..." "I mean,..."; "Actually,..."; or "Do you know what I mean?"

31. A: Naming interviews are seen as an activity that helps affirm students' identities because names are often deeply rooted in culture. Names hold value within a culture and are associated with certain meanings. By allowing students to discuss this in the classroom, students are able to bring an important aspect of themselves—their names—to light. Although show and tell can be culturally affirming, it doesn't necessarily have to do with a student's cultural identity. Activities that validate students' cultural identities should focus on the student.

32. A: The eavesdropper is likely engaging in pragmatics. Pragmatics examines how speakers' linguistic understanding depends upon external context, how meaning can be found in the confluence of the rules of a language—its grammar, vocabulary, idioms, and so forth—and contextual information that is not embedded in the language itself, such as inferences, spatial relationships, and so forth.

33. B: The Cognitive Academic Language Learning Approach (CALLA) and Specially Designed Academic Instruction in English (SDAIE) and other sheltered-English approaches feature using content-area instruction as a vehicle for language instruction. English for a specific purpose (ESP) is a very specialized branch of English instruction, which is focused less on generalized English skills and more on acquiring vocabulary and other useful language for particular purposes like business, science, or a particular vocation. ESP is more specialized than just academic language. Direct instruction refers to teaching English directly without use of the first language as a platform. Direct

Instruction is a highly structured, teacher-centered model that emphasizes explicit teaching and guided practice of skills, and it is not organized around content-area instruction as the vehicle for language development. Total physical response (TPR) is an approach that involves adding action into the instruction, including movement and application of actions to help with grounding the language in the real world. CALLA and SDAIE are both types of approaches to language learning that focus on academic content as the primary driver for language learning opportunities. While they are both content-based, they do also address generalized English skills to promote accurate, formal uses of language, and not just practical skills which are applied to a narrow subject.

34. A: Social language-learning strategies include requesting clarification, repetition, or elaboration to enhance comprehension. In learning languages, students use these to make up for language deficits like unfamiliarity with certain linguistic structures or vocabulary words a speaker uses and to comprehend meanings in new or different contexts. The teacher's practice promotes the English language learner (ELL) students' development of social language-learning strategies. Directing them to request repetition or clarification does not specifically raise grammatical awareness (B) or apply cognitive processes for internalizing language (D). The Zone of Proximal Development (C) is the area wherein students can accomplish learning tasks with assistance from one who knows more than they could independently. Because the presenters and listeners are all ELL students in the same class, no one is assisting another, and listeners' requesting repetition or clarification does not imply any presenter necessarily knows more than any listener.

35. B: The student constructs English sentences this way because, in German, the student's L1, it is common to construct sentences with the verb at the end, whereas in English, the verb typically comes before any objects that it modifies (e.g., the indirect object "to the class"). The student has transferred German syntax to English. This example has nothing to do with a lack of vocabulary (A), English verb conjugations versus German verb inflections (C), or differences between languages in the present progressive tense (D), which does not exist in German (neither does the past progressive; time expressions, e.g., "at this time" or "at that time," and so on, are added).

36. B: Indicating one picture among several to answer questions is a way that English language learners (ELLs) at beginning proficiency levels can show their content knowledge and their receptive (listening) understanding of English (A) without being penalized by having inadequate expressive (speaking) English skills interfere (C); these are advantages. Because picture selection is a receptive response mode, there is no risk they will communicate incorrect or unclear meanings through incorrect word choice (D), another advantage. The only listed limitation of this response method is that, by responding without speaking, students have no way to elaborate upon or explain their responses further (B).

37. B: The law requires schools to notify parents of the reasons they identified their child for participation in an ESL program and of the need for placing the child in the ESL program. They must also notify parents of both their child's level of English proficiency and how they assessed this level (A), as well as the status of their child's academic achievement (D), the instructional methods they use in their ESL program, and also how their ESL program will meet the child's educational needs (C).

38. D: One way to help involve English language learner (ELL) parents with their children's school is to contact other parents with similar socioeconomic and cultural profiles and recruit their help in furthering positive home–school communication. Parent liaisons can offer communication and instruction to other ELL families and community members. Another effective educator strategy is to be open to meeting with parents outside of normal school hours and locations to accommodate parental limitations with childcare, transportation, and work schedules. Other cultures can have very different school systems, so educators often need to teach them about the collaborative, communicative style of American school cultures, or parents will feel unsure about how they can participate actively in children's educations at schools. Researchers also find educators must connect immigrant families with businesses and community programs to help meet their basic needs before family school involvement can succeed.

39. D: Academic essays include different text structures, for example, comparison–contrast, problem–solution, logical sequence, attributive, and so on. Giving English language learner (ELL) students examples of these and helping them analyze the essays will familiarize them with the organization, characteristics, and parts of different essay types; helping them make graphic organizers that visually illustrate the various essay types' structures will not only acquaint them with essay formats but will also give them tools they can refer to for writing their own essays. Answer choice A would give writing practice but no exposure to existing academic essay types. Answer choice B would give practice with vocabulary using contextual cues but no familiarity with academic essay text structures. Answer choice C would help ELLs compare but not differentiate essay types.

40. C: English language learner (ELL) students should have text analysis and interpretation assignments as part of Specially Designed Academic Instruction in English (SDAIE) lessons in both written and oral form to develop the listening, speaking, and writing as well as reading domains of English language development (ELD). Therefore, these assignments should not be limited to writing (A) or listening and speaking (B). Individual oral exams with the teacher (D) with the excuse of avoiding student embarrassment will deprive them of the experience and practice they need with using conversational and academic English to listen and speak, that is, communicate, with their peers as well as their teachers.

41. A: To develop English language learner (ELL) students' academic English in content-based English language development (ELD) instruction, the teacher needs to expose them to the maximum comprehensible English print materials possible. Selecting a grade-level text will ensure they are learning content appropriate to fifth grade. Adapting the syntax and vocabulary of the textbook to student English language proficiency (ELP) levels will make it comprehensible to them while also furthering their development of academic English. Avoiding print (B) will not give enough written English exposure. Substituting an outline for text (C) also limits print exposure. Selecting a lower grade-level text (D) will not provide appropriate grade-level content.

42. A: Phonology is the study of sound patterns as it relates to language. This teacher's activity focuses on phonemes that are part of the English language but may not be present in other languages. This is often confused with phonetics, which is the study of specific speech sounds without context and does not require prior knowledge. Morphology is the study of the meaning of language units, whereas syntax is focused on sentence structure and formation.

43. B: Peer tutoring would likely be the easiest method to implement in order to support the ELLs. With peer tutoring, the students at higher ELP levels can tutor those at lower levels. Technology is a significant support to supplement teacher instruction and facilitate all kinds of student activities; however, choosing, procuring, and training on new technology would be more difficult to accomplish than peer tutoring. Team teaching and paraprofessionals can be helpful, but peer tutoring is generally preferred if viable.

44. B: The ESL teacher has advocated for the new student in all of these ways. The teacher has facilitated parental involvement in their child's education (A) by securing an interpreter to overcome language barriers and having the local center's staff help explain American cultural and school practices. The teacher has accomplished communication and collaboration with the parents (C) by enlisting their participation in school activities once their intimidation has been reduced and they are more receptive to involvement. The teacher has also accessed available community resources (D) to accomplish these other things by contacting the local community center to obtain the interpreter and additional cross-cultural supports.

45. B: Lana is categorizing irregular verbs as both different—i.e., in a different category—from regular verbs, and as the same—i.e., falling into the same category—as certain other irregular verbs. In this example, she has not memorized these similarities and differences (A), but simply observed them. She has not generalized (C) across all verbs, but made distinctions between and within categories. She is not thinking about her own cognitive processes (D), but using them to think about the language.

46. C: Assigning cooperative group learning activities allows students of different backgrounds the highest levels of interaction for the most culturally inclusive learning environment. Assigning students to homogeneous groups with similar backgrounds (A) reduces interaction with students from other backgrounds. Assigning independent activities to prevent cultural conflicts (B) eliminates learning interactions with students from diverse backgrounds. Assigning students to fixed pairs to expose each student to one partner's different background (D) limits each student to learning interactions with only one other student from a different background, instead of with many other students from different backgrounds.

47. D: Summative assessments are used to evaluate students' learning at the end of a unit, semester, school year, or other extended period of time. The remaining options describe formative assessments, which are given throughout the learning process and used to plan or adapt instruction during the unit based on students' performances.

48. B: The teacher initially attributed the student's attitude to either linguistic or personal issues and overlooked the possibility of cultural causes because of her own cultural values, beliefs, and assumptions. This is why it is important for educators to examine their own cultural attitudes and what impacts they have on teaching culturally diverse students. Ignorance about the student's home culture (A) was a secondary reason; however, even not knowing about it, the teacher would more likely consider culture as a reason initially or investigate cultural reasons first were it not for her own cultural assumptions. The question does not include any information about the teacher's own childhood history (C). Knowing the student as a person (D) might or might not show the teacher the student was otherwise self-confident or comfortable with English-language speaking, but only by examining her own cultural assumptions could she consider culture as informing the student's attitude.

49. A: This is mostly an example of using the student's prior knowledge of his native language to promote English language development. The teacher points out and lists L1–L2 cognates, showing same and similar spellings and different pronunciations. The similarity of cognates reinforces Jose's ability to add new English vocabulary words through his familiarity with the Spanish versions of the same words. Explaining and modeling the pronunciation differences help him make adjustments for correctly articulating the English versions. This is not an example of teaching decoding skills (B) as the teacher is not showing him specifically how to associate English letters with English phonemes. It is not systematic phonics instruction (C) for the same reason. It is not applying word analysis (D) because they are not breaking the words down into their component parts or discussing their etymologies.

50. D: The definition of sensitivity in a test instrument is how often (typically measured in percentages) it accurately identifies a specific problem or disorder that it is designed to identify, e.g., a mental health disorder, a developmental delay, or a learning disability. If tests either over-identify or under-identify problems that are its targets (A), these are measurement errors rather than levels of sensitivity. Sensitivity in screening does not refer to adverse effects of a test on the person being tested (B), though this is a separate ethical concern if the test is harmful to the test cases. Sensitivity does not mean ruling out (C) a targeted condition. How often a test rules out a problem is often referred to as specificity.

51. A: Lack of communication does not always mean disengagement or lack of caring. Different cultures may have different levels of parental involvement in schooling and may have gendered roles for who is responsible for a child's education. Answer C does not seem to be the answer because the scenario depicts Amal's mother being involved despite his father being uninvolved. Furthermore, although language barriers may be a factor that has to be considered, this deferral to the mother indicates possible gender roles within the culture.

52. B: The teacher should involve her students in a series of physical activities in response to her instructions and requests. Total Physical Response (TPR) employs physical involvement to make learning more meaningful and easier to retain. A sequence of instructions given by the teacher prompts a succession of detailed actions. Advocates recommend special hands-on training with a trained senior instructor.

53. C: The teacher should invite several parents from the same or similar cultures to work with their children and a translator if one is available. and she should create a classroom presentation on some cultural aspect that will be of interest to the students. For example, Mexican and other Central American parents might present a slideshow on the Day of the Dead, followed by a show-and-tell of objects used in that celebration.

54. D: Although refreshments can be a nice touch, they are not an essential part of parent–teacher conferences. It is important for schools and teachers to consider having an interpreter if parents do not speak English. Moreover, there may be cultural differences in perceptions of time as well as of involvement in schools. It is important to communicate these expectations and create alternatives to allow for these cultural differences. Furthermore, some families may be working during the school day, making it difficult for parents to come to school during that time. This doesn't apply to only English learners but all learners.

55. D: Extended time is most likely the best accommodation to offer the student. Extended time on assessments is often necessary for English language learners because of the additional time needed to process language. By reducing the word problems to mere calculations, the teacher is changing the nature of the examination and may not be assessing the same skills as in the original examination. In addition, if the student is able to use his or her notes, he or she may not show an understanding of formulas that the teacher is testing.

56. D: Simultaneous bilingualism refers to when an individual learns two languages at the same time. This may occur in bilingual schools in which the individual is exposed to two languages or when a home has two different languages being spoken. Sequential bilingualism, on the other hand, refers to languages that were learned one after the other. This is often how students learn a second language.

57. D: Memorization (A) by itself would not explain this process. While learners might memorize past tense or past perfect tense endings for regular verbs as *-ed,* applying the memorized morpheme to irregular verbs is itself not memorization. It does not reflect categorization (B) but rather a lack of it, for example, classifying verbs as regular or irregular and including irregular forms under the latter category. Generalization (C) involves correctly applying the regular verb ending to regular verbs. However, incorrectly applying regular verb endings to irregular verbs is an instance of overgeneralization (D), that is, extending the rule too far to include a category that should not be included.

58. B: By employing a variety of learning activities, assignments, and teaching strategies according to the differing needs of diverse students, a teacher helps to establish an inclusive learning environment. Using a single teaching method with all students (A) will not address their different backgrounds, experiences, skills, and learning styles. Rather than devoting a single class to studying cultural diversity (C), teachers can teach more inclusively by integrating diversity throughout the entire curriculum. To teach inclusively, teachers can intentionally establish safer learning environments by setting and enforcing some ground rules for students rather than not having any (D).

59. C: An effective strategy for intercultural interactions is to keep an open mind for accepting new information that is not familiar about a culture or cultural group. It is a common human ethnocentric habit to disregard or distort information that does not fit into existing worldviews. Another effective strategy is not generalizing from one area of an individual's competence or incompetence to all other areas (A). For example, just because somebody speaks poor English does not indicate that he or she is generally incompetent. Rather than being honest about discomfort with people from other cultures (B), it is better to keep one's normal discomfort from making one treat those people differently. While acknowledging to oneself that some discomfort with people from unfamiliar cultures is natural, it is important not to treat them unfairly or with favoritism. It is not considerate or a way to avoid embarrassing others not to explain cultural expectations (D): People from other cultures cannot figure out our unwritten cultural rules, so one must expect having to explain these, even if it is embarrassing or uncomfortable.

60. C: Rubrics are an effective tool to help teachers grade an assessment consistently from student to student. Well constructed rubrics have strong reliability scores as they help define objective measures for scoring potentially subjective assessments, such as essays or presentations. Rubrics can be helpful in communicating expectations and guiding learning when they are used to communicate expectations to students; however, not all teachers provide the scoring rubric to students, as this can skew the results of certain types of assessments.

61. B: The Student Study Team (SST) (A) would determine if a student's school difficulties were caused by learning disabilities; medical, physical, psychological, social, or other problems; or language barriers. It is already known this student knows no English, and the specialist has identified very high IQ and adaptive functioning in his L1 but no disabilities. Hence, a special education (C) referral or other intervention programs (D) are not indicated. A Gifted and talented education (GATE) (B) referral is indicated because this student's IQ and other scores show he is intellectually and adaptively gifted or talented.

62. C: English language learner (ELL) students having intellectual disabilities and specific learning disabilities will have different cognitive needs than ELL students without these cognitive disabilities. Being in the same class, these students will not necessarily have different academic needs as they will all be held to the same academic standards and benchmarks regardless of how their teacher helps them to meet these. Even if their L1s and English language proficiency (ELP) levels differ, all of their linguistic needs are still to develop grade-level ELP. Not enough information is provided to know whether their cultural needs differ; however, the information given clearly identifies differing cognitive needs for several students.

63. C: Reading aloud portions or chunks of the texts they are using for the unit to the entire class is a good strategy to differentiate instruction for the English language learner (ELL) students in the class while maintaining inclusive teaching. Differentiated instruction should include both homogeneous (A) and heterogeneous (B) grouping of ELL students—not only one or the other—to promote both team behaviors and participation by every student, respectively. Another differentiated instruction strategy to help ELL students is to use sticky notes, highlighting (D), and other ways of annotating the texts throughout to develop content-area vocabulary, teach more difficult words, encourage student inquiry and questioning, and enhance ELL student reading comprehension.

64. B: Affective filter is activated when students are stressed, or their self-esteem is lowered. Teachers should create a supportive environment with constructive feedback to help students learn while lowering their affective filters. Having students work together in small groups provides a supportive and low-pressure setting for sharing ideas and receiving feedback. Correcting every mistake is often harmful for English learners at the beginning level as production is more important than precision at that stage. Cold-calling students can also heighten anxiety for students; however, ignoring students completely create an environment in which these learners are not included. Students may perceive this as English learners being less valued in the class.

65. B: The Bilingual Syntax Measure is a tool designed to assess bilingual students for oral language proficiency and dominance between two languages. Its reliability has been debated since its development.

66. D: In a longitudinal study of electronic teacher feedback provided to English language learner (ELL) students, researchers found it equally explicit and systematic (A) as handwritten feedback; equally effective at evoking student revisions (B) to improve content, organization, grammatical structure, and surface characteristics; and equally based on student needs (C). Hence, electronic feedback was found neither inferior nor superior to handwritten feedback but similar and equally effective. The authors concluded that electronic feedback should not be avoided.

67. D: Textbook examinations are those that are provided by the textbook publisher. They often align closely with the content of the textbook and can be more aligned with the state standards and in this case the advanced placement class objectives. This type of test can cover all of the requirements that students must cover for the course. Unfortunately, it often is rigid and does not allow for students' opinions, backgrounds, and cultures. Answer A describes a portfolio assessment in which students have the opportunity to be assessed on pieces of work rather than on one examination. Although this type of assessment may be easier to grade, that should not be the main consideration for choosing an assessment.

68. C: BICS stands for basic interpersonal communication skills, which are language skills that focus on social situations. People generally learn BICS quickly in several months, even for a second language. On the other hand, cognitive academic language proficiency (CALP) often takes 7 to 10 years to develop. This language skill is used in academic settings, such as the classroom, and it is highly formal, complex, and decontextualized. Syntactic knowledge refers to the patterns that govern sentence construction. For example, "A bird flies" follows the syntactic patterns of English, whereas "Flies a bird" does not. This is different from semantics, which is the study of the meaning of words and phrases.

69. B: Displaying objectives for language development is a key aspect to Specially Designed Academic Instruction in English (SDAIE) in all subjects. Although modifying texts may be appropriate depending on the students' levels, it is important to adapt the text in a way that makes the language more accessible without simplifying the content. In addition, although figurative language and idioms can be difficult for English learners, it is essential, especially at the early-advanced level to expose students to these concepts and help build their knowledge of idioms. Organizers are often a great way to support students' reading comprehension; however, at the early-advanced level, fill-in-the-blanks assignments may be too easy. Instead, an organizer that provides headings and subheadings with spaces for students to write their own summaries and notes would be more appropriate for this level.

70. A: According to experts, seven parameters to use as guidelines for transforming school curriculum to be multicultural are countries, cultures, and lives of origin; histories of oppression (B); works and contributions; implementers (C) and designers; global inclusiveness as well as local responsiveness (D); autobiographical (C) foundations; and student agency, social action, and authorship.

71. D: The sheltered English instruction program model can accommodate all English-language proficiency levels of ESL students. It affords flexibility and is content-based. Therefore it would be the most suitable program model for this district with its high student diversity. Early-exit (A) or late-exit (B) bilingual program models would not be feasible because the ESL students in this district speak too many different native languages to implement a bilingual program. The model of pull-out classes (C) is limited to elementary schools with small numbers of ESL students, so it would not be suitable for district-wide implementation.

72. C: Building literacy skills in all content areas will improve CALP and increase language and abstract thinking skills across the board. Cognitive Academic Language Proficiency requires specialized vocabularies for specific content areas and the ability to apply abstract concepts to areas that are not transparently related.

73. C: When assessing typically developing English language learner (ELL) students in their first languages, a consideration is that, as ELLs (unless very newly arrived), they have recently had less exposure to their L1s and more to English. Consequently, their L1 skills may be at an earlier level of development or have deteriorated with time. This puts them at risk of being overidentified as having developmental disorders or delays affecting language development. Additional considerations for L1 assessment is that standardized instruments are not as available here in L1s as they are in English (A); qualified practitioners to assess in L1s rather than English are also less available (B). ELLs are not as likely to be under-identified with language disorders or delays (D) as overidentified (C) when assessed in their L1s.

74. A: The first thing the teacher must do is to assess the student's language proficiency level. She cannot assume his proficiency is reflected by his understanding and speech of English because social English develops much sooner and more rapidly than academic language and will not help him succeed academically without academic English language proficiency. The teacher also must assess the student's proficiency level to know where to begin English language instruction. Assessing the student's previous L1 knowledge, giving the student scaffolding for language tasks, and monitoring the student's English language progress are all things the teacher can do during instruction after she assesses his level of English language proficiency, which will inform these practices.

75. D: Clauses consist of subjects and predicates. Independent clauses are those that can stand on their own as a sentence and can be described as a complete thought, whereas a dependent clause requires an independent clause and cannot be a sentence on its own. While giving examples and having students understand the differences is important, the first step would be to define clauses.

76. A: Front-loading vocabulary means that the teacher is pre-teaching key words that are part of a reading. This strategy helps improve comprehension because students have a better understanding of key concepts that are introduced in the passage. Front-loading builds rather than reduces schemata or background knowledge. It may improve communication skills but does not necessarily relate to interpersonal language skills. Front-loading vocabulary does not necessarily support diverse learning styles that require multiple modalities.

77. B: Presenting sufficient and meaningful reading and writing experiences for students to practice strategies and reviewing and re-teaching as required to ensure that students have integrated essential content are part of scientifically-based, quality classroom instruction. Daily introduction to new concepts, words, and materials can be okay as long as they are integrated a little at a time. Students require multiple exposures to a word before recognition begins to happen automatically. This relies on Krashen's input hypothesis, which states that learners benefit from exposure to slightly more difficult language than their current level. This renders answer choice B as the least effective, since it implies only using a level of language that the student is comfortable with.

78. A: NCLB provides that federal funds are to be used to supplement federal, state, or local public funds for ESL programs. It specifies under Section 3115 (g) that such funds be *only* supplementary rather than supplanting (replacing) federal, state, or local public funds, stating that Title III should NOT be used as the main budget to fund an ESL program (B); to pay for required FTE positions that would otherwise be funded with state or local dollars (C); or to run programs without other sources of funding (D).

79. C: Physical contact and distance between speakers is highly cultural. Some cultures use frequent physical contact when talking with one another, whereas other cultures maintain distance and feel awkward or embarrassed when physical contact occurs. It is important to keep this in mind when dealing with students from different cultural backgrounds. This behavior from the student may not necessarily mean that there is physical abuse occurring at home or that the speaker has any particular feelings toward the teacher.

80. A: Plyler v. Doe was the 1982 Supreme Court case that established the right to a free education for undocumented immigrant children. In 1975, Texas laws were revised, permitting districts to refuse to enroll illegal alien children. The Supreme Court used this case to strike down the Texas law, finding it in violation of the 14th Amendment, which gives equal rights to all people.

81. A: Balanced reading programs combine different aspects of reading that include phonics, fluency, and comprehension, among other reading skills. Although vocabulary and fluency are both important, the balanced reading approach looks at all of these skills as important rather than building a single skill, such as Answers C and D suggest. Using student stories for literacy can be a form of the Language Experience Approach.

82. C: Graphic organizers are visual representations of concepts, words, or other learning matter. As such, they help English language learner (ELL) students, students with reading-related learning disabilities, students with cognitive deficits, and others who may have difficulty accessing verbal information. Learning logs (A) typically use written language and hence are verbal or linguistic in nature. Shared reading (B) requires students to read written language together with peers or others, and thus is linguistic in nature. Interactive journals (D) allow students to think independently and creatively, process classroom information, and express their own ideas. While these typically include pictures and other nonlinguistic elements, they typically also involve writing and include words. Hence, of these choices, graphic organizers are typically the most visual and nonlinguistic.

83. D: Culturally supportive classes are those that are inclusive of all cultural backgrounds. Some key aspects of these kinds of classes include high expectations; however, it is important to balance high expectations with realistic ones, such as ensuring that each student has ample time to formulate responses. Using high-level academic vocabulary that is inaccessible for students can create frustration and confusion. Furthermore, culturally supportive classrooms allow for the use of the primary language to support learning. Finally, modifying and differentiating activities for learners is important, but it should not lead to oversimplifying all activities for English learners.

84. A: Debriefing is a cognitive or metacognitive strategy wherein the teacher helps English language learners (ELLs) develop more autonomy in learning by guiding them carefully to reflect on what and how they learned and to use metacognition to analyze the cognitive processes they used in performing learning tasks. Hence, debriefing involves reflection. However, reflection does not necessarily always involve debriefing (B). Students may reflect on their learning independently or as assigned by their teacher but without the guidance of debriefing. Another metacognitive strategy teachers can instruct students in explicitly is to use text features; however, debriefing does not require this (C). Debriefing is not equal to self-evaluation (D): In self-evaluation, for example, students might complete a teacher-made checklist showing which learning tasks they accomplished, rating how well they did them, and so on.

85. C: This student was raised in a collectivist culture typical of many Asian, Latin American, and other countries. American culture is individualistic, valuing competition and individual expression; collectivist cultures value cooperation above competition, often disapprove of individual expression outside of cultural norms, and advocate deferring one's own needs for the sake of group harmony and furthering the common good. Whereas the individual is paramount in the United States, in collectivist cultures, the group takes precedence. Rather than being intimidated, wanting to please her peers (A), trying to make new friends (B), or feeling inferior and afraid to compete (D) as motives, the most likely cultural reason for this student's behavior is to conform to the values of her native culture.

86. B: These educator practices demonstrate their awareness that students are more likely to develop English language proficiency when their families have more positive attitudes toward school and learning. Choice (A) is incorrect because parents who are not native English speakers may not know enough about the English language specifically to instruct children in English. Choice (C) is incorrect because ESL students' families may not have enough ELP to model purposeful English communication. Choice (D) is incorrect because the school district is responsible, rather than students' families, for evaluating the effectiveness of the school's language instruction.

87. B: Authentic assessment techniques are designed to build higher-order thinking skills because they require students to construct their own answers instead of choosing from preselected answers. They also allow for the possibility that multiple "correct" answers are possible because students bring different perspectives and prior experiences to the material. They typically measure student performance over an extended period of time and are graded on a criterion-referenced basis (e.g., students are compared to an objective standard, rather than being directly compared to one another).

88. A: Euphoria is the initial stage that individuals generally experience due to the excitement of being in a new culture. Cultural fatigue and culture shock are the same stage in which newcomers are disoriented and frustrated by the difference between cultures. The final stage is adjustment, which is sometimes known as adaptation. This is when the individual adjusts to the new culture and is able to successfully integrate into the dominant culture.

89. A: Krashen advocates letting students produce utterances in the new language when they are ready rather than forcing them to produce early (B), correcting their production (C), drilling extensively, or consciously applying grammar rules (D). He finds learning depends on meaningful interactions in the L2, wherein learners are more concerned with the content they hear and express than with the form of what they say.

90. D: Although all of these actions promote cultural diversity in the school, the best way to encourage this goal is through training teachers and changing the curriculum to be more inclusive. Posters and monthly multicultural events may have some impact and should be done, but it is a more surface-level change that would not enhance cultural diversity deeply in the school. Having parent and community members speak would also support diversity, but it should be integrated into the curriculum rather than be standalone events. Training teachers and changing the curriculum would have a daily effect on students, whereas the other actions may be less frequent.

91. C: The error is in subject–verb agreement. The student has included two subjects, "understanding spoken English" and "speaking in English," so the verb should be the plural *are* rather than the singular *is*. There is nothing wrong with the word order (A) or the verb tense (B), only thc number. Thus (D) is incorrect.

92. C: The student is engaging in categorization by assigning different classes to (1) regular verbs that take the *-ed* ending for past and past perfect tenses and (2) certain (not all) irregular verbs that undergo the same /i/, /o/, /o-ɛn/ vowel changes for these tenses. It is not memorization (A) because she is observing and classifying, but not memorizing, two groups of verb conjugation types. It is not generalization (B) because she differentiates between two classes of verb types with different conjugated forms. It would be generalization if she learned only the *-ed* rule for all regular verbs or learned only the vowel change rule for all included irregular verbs. It is not overgeneralization (D): If she misapplied the regular *-ed* ending to the irregular verbs that would be overgeneralization (also called overregularization when it involves applying regular verb endings to irregular verbs).

93. D: The question in (A) requires only factual knowledge, that is, remembering (or looking up) and reciting the seven names of noble gases. Question (B) requires this same factual knowledge plus being able to categorize gases and differentiate noble gases from other kinds. Question (C) is similar to question (B) but is also outdated and inaccurate for using the term *inert*: Noble gases historically were considered inert but today are deemed relatively inert, that is, extremely stable and nonreactive, but it is not completely impossible for them to form compounds as previously thought. Question (D) requires the most critical thinking because students must apply knowledge of the stability of noble gases to answer "easy" or "hard" and then must additionally explain why, that is, because their octets or valence shells are filled with the maximum numbers of electrons, making them very stable and thus resistant to compounding. This question requires analysis, application, and interpretation as well as factual knowledge.

94. D: One way to reach out to parents lacking English language skills is informing them of learning opportunities in the community they can pursue, including English and native language literacy courses, parenting courses, family literacy projects, and others. Teachers can ask school administrators to research, compile, and regularly update lists of such resources, available in both English and parents' native languages. Learning even a few common words and phrases in the parents' language does much good (A) by making them feel welcome and showing the teacher is making the effort to communicate. Teachers should find fully bilingual adult interpreters rather than use the student (B), which can make parents feel disempowered. Monolingual teachers can give parents contact information for bilingual staff members. This is not passing parents off (C) but providing them with additional resource people to discuss educational issues in their language. Teachers also can give parents contacts for other parents speaking their language to help each other and share their experiences. Asking parents able and willing to volunteer is also beneficial.

95. A: Dialects are regional or social varieties of a language that differ in pronunciation, vocabulary, or grammar but are generally mutually intelligible. Hindi and Urdu are treated as separate languages for cultural and historical reasons, although they are mutually intelligible in everyday speech. Chinese "dialects" are often classified that way for historical and political reasons and are not mutually intelligible and are considered separate languages. Common examples of true dialects include differences in language due to region, such as New York City and Los Angeles, or social varieties like African American Vernacular English and Southern United States English.

96. A: The student has used procedural memory, that is, the type of memory for managing the application of grammatical rules to produce language. Having just learned the new English vocabulary word *focus,* she is additionally able to generate the past tense *focused* and the participle *focusing* because she has learned the English grammar rules for adding *–ed* to create past tense with regular verbs and *–ing* to create the progressive participle. Declarative (B) memory is the kind of memory that would enable her to recall previously learned vocabulary words, phrases, and sentences along with their meanings and other facts, knowledge, and concepts rather than to transform words grammatically by applying rules. Semantic (C) memory is the subtype of declarative memory used to remember vocabulary words, facts, and so on. Episodic (D) memory is the subtype of declarative memory used to remember personal experiences, events, and associated emotions.

97. A: The No Child Left Behind Act of 2001 required that for schools to receive federal funding, they must measure and report student achievement on standardized tests for all students, including English learners. This includes state assessments. The Every Student Succeeds Act (ESSA), passed in 2015, gave states flexibility in how to measure and report achievement rather than using a prescribed measure from the federal government.

98. B: Simply including diverse literature in the curriculum is not enough to create an inclusive environment. Many "diverse" books can include stereotypical depictions of minority characters, including women. Although having multiple translations can be helpful, it is not essential when thinking about what texts to choose to teach. Well-known authors may be beneficial as it can draw the interest of students, but it is not required, and considering the author for a talk at the school depends on the funding available, which may not always be possible.

99. A: Behavioral theorists believe that the mind is a "blank slate" and that students learn exactly what has been taught by the teacher. This method focuses on reinforcement through repetition and using rewards or punishments to support behavior. The main focus is on teacher output and a focus on student behaviors in response to the teacher.

100. A: Phonemes are the individual, smallest breakdown of sounds in a language. Not all languages have the same phonemes, and this can pose a challenge to English learners. Phonemic awareness is the ability to hear, identify, and manipulate individual sounds (phonemes) in spoken words. A rime is the vowel and any following consonants in a syllable; in both 'sap' and 'tap' the rime is -ap. Practicing minimal pairs like 'sap' and 'tap' draws students' attention to the one sound that changes the word, which strengthens their ability to hear and distinguish different phonemes in English.

Practice Test #2

1. For a teacher of English language learner (ELL) students, including which of the following would be the MOST effective use of Specially Designed Academic Instruction in English (SDAIE) lessons?

a. Assigning reading and writing tasks in English language development (ELD) classes and oral presentations and discussions in social studies classes
b. Assigning reading and writing tasks in math and science classes and oral presentations and discussions in ELD classes
c. Assigning reading and writing, oral presentations, and discussions in ELD and math, science, and social studies
d. Assigning only reading and writing in all classes with scaffolding until students have reached higher oral English language proficiency (ELP) levels

2. In the history of education, which accurately describes how ESL students were addressed before World War II in American school systems?

a. Only the largest city school systems offered ESL programs for their education.
b. Non-English-speaking students' school enrollment could be legally prohibited.
c. American schools had no system-wide initiatives to help educate ESL students.
d. Most ESL students having low LEP were educated in bilingual parochial schools.

3. Which of the following is a software program that would most benefit an English language learner (ELL) student for learning to speak English like a native?

a. The English as a second language (ESL Jobs Forum)
b. The Reading Plus system
c. Rosetta Stone's software
d. Software For Students' Easy Writer

4. A fourth-grade English Language Development (ELD) teacher is planning on conducting writing workshops with her students to develop narrative texts in which students write stories that incorporate their culture. What first step for students would best support the writing workshop approach?

a. Drafting topic sentences with the use of teacher-provided word walls and word banks
b. Sharing experiences with classmates in small groups to generate ideas
c. Using sentence stems provided by the teacher to begin writing
d. Learning grammatical structures that will be used in the narrative texts

5. To foster good teacher–student relationships between the teacher and all students, which action should a teacher avoid?

a. Convey equality and commitment toward all students.
b. Change the level of physical contact based on the student's cultural norms.
c. Allow students to discuss their feelings and personal lives.
d. Communicate acceptance toward all students.

6. The ESL teacher has several students with little knowledge of English. How can she best help them develop English competency?

a. Drill verb cases; build vocabulary with a word wall; read the same books repeatedly to build their semantic understanding
b. Incorporate extra-linguistic materials into instruction, such as realia, gestures, and enactments (increased comprehensibility, contextual clues)
c. Have them listen and repeat exercises from a language CD; teach them a "word of the day" and ask them to use it five times in oral or written communication; praise them when they are successful
d. Invite members of a mainstreamed age-appropriate class to visit, and assign each child to a mainstreamed "mentor" to share conversations on topics the ESL children offer

7. An English Language Development (ELD) teacher notices that one of his English learners is refusing to use his home language in school. He has started to hang out with native English speakers and dressing similarly to them. What is this phenomenon known as?

a. Accommodation
b. Biculturalism
c. Culture shock
d. Assimilation

8. For placement decision purposes, a small school is trying to determine the English language proficiency of a student who speaks fluent English but has no knowledge of academic English for any of the subject content areas. Important contributions to their decision-making process are made by their ESL teacher. This is an example of:

a. The ESL teacher's contribution to the ARD meeting.
b. The ESL teacher's serving on the SBDM committee.
c. The ESL teacher's participation on the school's LPAC.
d. The ESL teacher's serving as a resource for teachers.

9. Which of the following is a common criticism that has been leveled at oral proficiency assessments, such as the Language Assessment Scales-Oral, the Woodcock-Muñoz Language Survey, and the IDEA Proficiency Test?

a. They are biased toward native English speakers.
b. They are biased toward non-native English speakers.
c. They do not accurately reflect native speakers' academic performance and therefore cannot accurately reflect non-native speakers' performance.
d. They do not accurately reflect native speakers' proficiency and therefore cannot accurately reflect non-native speakers' proficiency.

10. A teacher seeks to increase the self-esteem of students to help them succeed in the classroom. She praises students for effort, creates a culture of positive language, and allows for differences of opinion. Which factor related to language learning is she developing?

a. Affective
b. Cognitive
c. Political
d. Sociocultural

11. Which of the following is an example of scaffolding content-area assessment tasks for English language learner (ELL) students?

a. Providing ELL students with a glossary of English chemistry terms to write their experiment report
b. Providing ELL students with an English thesaurus while they write a descriptive essay for ELA class
c. Providing ELL students with guiding questions and writing models for their narrative compositions
d. Providing ELL students with pictures for reference in responding with vocabulary word definitions

12. Which of the following is true regarding the involvement of the community in schools and classrooms?

a. It is appropriate for the community to offer their insights about various cultural traditions but not religious traditions.
b. It is appropriate for the community to offer their insights about various linguistic traditions but not content expertise.
c. It is appropriate for the community to offer their insights about various cultures and languages but not content expertise.
d. It is appropriate for the community to offer their insights about various cultures, languages, and content expertise.

13. According to research findings, which of these is true about second-language development?

a. Students lacking previous L1 formal education take longer to develop social language in L2.
b. Students lacking previous L1 formal education take longer to develop L2 academic language.
c. Students transferring L1 features to the L2 always demonstrate negative language transfer.
d. Students transferring L1 features to the L2 always demonstrate positive language transfer.

14. An eighth-grade English teacher models think-aloud reading to her class, which includes several intermediate-level English language learners. She reads aloud a section of *The Giver*, pauses, and says, "This reminds me of a time when I had never seen snow and was flabbergasted when I saw it in real life for the first time. I was astonished at how soft and cold it was as it fell from the sky." What is the MOST likely purpose that the teacher had in using the think-aloud?

a. The activity will expand students' vocabulary through the use of words like *astonished* and *flabbergasted.*
b. The activity will help them learn how to use complex sentences that use subordinating conjunctions such as *when* and *as.*
c. The activity will improve students' listening skills, as they must pause in their reading to listen to something that is not written in the text.
d. The activity will model reading comprehension skills through the use of making connections to one's life.

15. To make multicultural instruction locally responsive, which of the following is correct?

a. Educators should share international experience in only general terms.
b. Educators should not ask students to share any personal perspectives.
c. Educators should share personal information relevant to class content.
d. Educators should incorporate student autobiographies, not their own.

16. In an integrated ESL rubric that integrates listening, speaking, reading, and writing, which of these would apply to an Advanced level rather than an Intermediate level?

a. Listening: Making assessments of descriptions and narrations of technical and factual material.
b. Speaking: Requesting and providing information/clarification for frequent misunderstandings.
c. Reading: Interpreting messages in both edited and authentic fictional prose on familiar topics.
d. Writing: Compound sentences using simple and continuous tenses of regular/irregular verbs.

17. Which of these is accurate about parent education classes that schools can offer to diverse families?

a. It is not the school's place to provide information about specific disabilities.
b. Schools should leave the prenatal care information to Planned Parenthood.
c. Schools can provide training in effective math, reading, and similar tutoring.
d. Only community agencies can offer information on aftercare opportunities.

18. A new teacher at a Navajo school notices that when he tries to play competitive games in the classroom, students are reluctant to participate. Which of the following offers a possible explanation for why this is the case?

a. Some cultures prioritize cooperation over competition.
b. The school does not allow for games during school, so students are not used to the activities.
c. There are not many games in Navajo culture.
d. The teacher is new, so the students don't want to show off and give a bad impression.

19. Among the following dimensions for differentiating instruction, which is usually the one associated with the teaching strategies MOST frequently used?

a. Complexity
b. Novelty
c. Depth
d. Pacing

20. Which of the following is an advantage of using anecdotal notes to assess student work?

a. Teachers can use these to collect information both during assessment and outside of it.
b. Unless a teacher adds norms or criteria for comparison, these notes lack standardization.
c. Teachers cannot record observations of individual student behaviors as with most tools.
d. Writing anecdotal notes can yield valuable insights but often lacks any supporting context.

21. Describe some cultural differences in how English language learners experience cultural contact in the educational contexts of student interactions and problem-solving and conflict-resolution processes. Describe an instructional approach to address these differences. Explain how this approach would be effective for addressing cultural differences.

22. When planning Specially Designed Academic Instruction in English (SDAIE) for middle-school English language learner (ELL) students with intermediate-level English language proficiency (ELP), which teacher approach is most applicable?

a. Integrating language objectives for content-specific structures and vocabulary in every algebra lesson
b. Giving ELLs more access to algebra lessons through skills and concepts at lower developmental levels
c. Putting off lessons involving more advanced algebra concepts until ELLs reach advanced receptive ELP
d. Planning lessons with minimal linguistic use, as math subjects rely less on language than others

23. Which of the following is an appropriate intercultural communication strategy?

a. Using Americanized names to make newcomers feel welcome
b. Using generalizations about cultural groups to know individuals
c. Finding out which terms cultural groups accept and using them
d. Maintaining the usual interpersonal space to show it is normal

24. A 12th-grade math teacher has a new English learner in her class. Ever since he arrived, she noticed that he tends to take longer than other students on activities and does not always adhere to the bell schedule. She thinks this is due to different cultural values around time. What is a modification she can provide for the student?

a. Change his schedule, so he has flexible classes.
b. Talk to the principal about this issue, so they can come up with a solution.
c. Allow for flexible timing of activities within her class period.
d. Pair the student with another student who can help speed up the work.

25. What should a teacher working with an ESL student who is at the preproduction stage do?

a. Devise role-playing games and activities.
b. Offer ample opportunity for face-to-face dialogue.
c. Encourage silent students to speak; this is especially important for introverted students.
d. Incorporate gesture, pictures, manipulatives, and other extra-verbal tools into her teaching.

26. A teacher preparing Specially Designed Academic Instruction in English (SDAIE) lessons for English language learner (ELL) students mainstreamed in an English-language class is planning small-group collaborative work to discuss their analyses and interpretations of English literature texts. What is the best way to group students for this assignment?

a. The ELL students should be grouped homogeneously to facilitate communication.
b. The ELL and native English-speaking students should be grouped heterogeneously.
c. The ELL students should be grouped heterogeneously but at least two per group.
d. The ELL and native English-speaking students' grouping will not make a difference.

27. Which of these is a definition of specificity in screening and assessment instruments?

a. A test's rate of correctly ruling out a disorder or delay
b. A test's rate of correctly identifying disorders or delay
c. A test's rate of identifying more issues than there are
d. A test's rate of identifying fewer issues than there are

28. Several English language learner (ELL) students in the same class came to America months before being enrolled in school. They acquired experience with conversing in English during the interim but have less experience and facility with reading written English. Which supplemental material or activity can the teacher provide that utilizes their proficiency with listening to English oral language to promote English literacy?

a. Providing lists of vocabulary words used in their reading with L1 translations
b. Providing audio recordings of books read aloud to accompany their reading
c. Providing text in English with the L1 translation of it for side-by-side reading
d. Providing paired reading assignments within the same group of ELL students

29. A veteran English Language Development (ELD) teacher notices that a new math teacher at the school has differentiated her homework for her English learners. English learners are asked to complete fewer math problems that still cover the same skills and concepts. What is an acceptable reason for the teacher to do this?

a. The math problems are difficult, so the teacher only assigns easy problems to the English language learners for them to be successful.
b. The math problems are language heavy, so English learners may take longer to complete the same number of problems.
c. The teacher knows that some of the English learners may not be able to complete the homework because a few of them have family obligations outside of school.
d. The teacher has fewer expectations of those students because of their language abilities.

30. A previously happy and affectionate ELL has suddenly become tearful and withdrawn. She reacts very strongly to any kind of unexpected touch, and she has abruptly stopped giving hugs to the teacher or to her friends. She will not tell the teacher what is causing her sadness or hurt, but the teacher is aware that the girl's mother has a new boyfriend who has recently moved in with the family. The student, who used to love writing in her journal both in Spanish and in English, now uses it only for drawings. The teacher has not violated the student's privacy by looking at the journal without permission, but she has noticed that during journal time the girl angrily scribbles what appear to be pictures of a man (or someone wearing a hat and pants) being shot, stabbed, or otherwise tortured. What should the teacher do?

a. Read the journal without permission; the girl is obviously disturbed, and if she is being abused in some way, the teacher has the responsibility to find out in any way possible.
b. Nothing at the moment; she should continue to observe the student and offer her an ear. Until the girl asks for help, she can legally do nothing.
c. Refer the student to the school counselor, who is trained to help in situations such as this.
d. Get the mother's permission to refer the student to the school counselor. She cannot be referred without parental permission.

31. ESL student Carlo has learned how some irregular English verbs are conjugated the same way, e.g., *freeze, froze, frozen* and *speak, spoke, spoken;* but he cannot fit *go, went, gone* into a group so easily. His strategy instead is to use______ with this and similar exceptions to the rules.

a. Categorization
b. Memorization
c. Generalization
d. Metacognition

32. A fifth-grade social studies teacher notices that one of her beginning-advanced English learners is having trouble with a unit on the American Revolution. This student is unable to write on what she knows about George Washington. Which factor is the most likely to affect second-language development in this context?

a. Psychological factors such as low self-esteem around language competence
b. A lack of prior knowledge of American history
c. Cultural factors such as not showing off what one knows
d. An underlying learning disability in memory or cognition

33. A second-grade English learner comes from a low socioeconomic background with parents who have not completed a middle school education. Her teacher notices that her parents are not involved in her schooling despite the class expectations that parents check over homework and read with the student. Which of the following explains why the parents do not get involved?

a. The family experiences cultural deprivation due to poverty.
b. The family is not interested in education.
c. The family holds different values on family involvement in education.
d. The family is uneducated, so they cannot read.

34. For a classroom activity, students are asked to interview one another about their interests. The teacher provides students with a list of follow-up questions and coaches them on how to show they are listening by using eye contact and nodding.

In this scenario, which language feature is the teacher focused on?

a. Semantics
b. Syntax
c. Discourse
d. Morphology

35. A Chinese student learning English tends to speak and write constructions like this: "This dish is my favorite because it has shrimp, snow pea, water chestnut, and bamboo shoot." To correct the errors represented in this sentence, what part of the English language does the teacher need to address?

a. morphology
b. phonology
c. semantics
d. syntax

36. An SDAIE approach can be problematic for an individual ESL teacher because it requires specialized training and is most effective when the program is adopted system wide. What strategy can such a teacher use to provide CBEC to her students without receiving that specialized training or having system wide support?

a. Determine the content areas that ESL students will be taught in the following semester and begin preparing them well in advance through a variety of approaches.
b. Teach concepts essential to a core understanding of the material that reach beyond just specialized vocabulary.
c. Organize learning thematically, and teach a series of interrelated, in-depth lessons related to that theme.
d. All the above

37. What is the main purpose of formative assessments?

a. To establish the background knowledge of students prior to beginning a unit
b. To assess students partway through a unit to establish which content is mastered and which needs to be retaught
c. To compare data to other teachers and assess the effectiveness of the teacher
d. To assess students at the conclusion of a unit of study

Refer to the following for question 38:

> A group of elementary intermediate-level English learners has difficulty identifying the differences between words like "there, they're, and their" as well as "eight and ate."

38. There/they're/their, eight/ate, and similar word pairs like shoe/shoo are:

a. Homophones
b. Synonyms
c. Homographs
d. Homonyms

39. For English language learner (ELL) students in kindergarten through Grade 1, which of the following strategies to scaffold tasks requiring academic language proficiency would be LEAST developmentally appropriate?

a. Realia
b. Analogies
c. Manipulatives
d. None of these would be developmentally appropriate.

40. An English language learner (ELL) student has grade-level English listening English skills and speaks English fluently but is two grades below grade level in reading English and three grades below grade level in writing English. Which would be the most appropriate teacher strategy to assess this student's mastery of grade-level objectives in subject content?

a. Use only authentic assessments.
b. Select from multiple strategies.
c. Scaffold all assessment tasks.
d. Use all written assessments.

41. In Wiggins and McTighe's backward design for designing instruction and assessment, in which stage are students expected to understand the big ideas (major concepts) in the unit being planned?

a. Stage 1
b. Stage 2
c. Stage 3
d. Stage 4

42. Which of the following describes how positive language transfer can be used in the classroom to support second-language learning?

a. Allowing group work to enhance communicative competence
b. Monitoring errors in vocabulary and grammar in writing
c. Using dual-language examples in the classroom to teach sentence structures
d. Teaching common prefixes and suffixes

43. Some schools feature ESL programs wherein full-time teachers give instruction that integrates academic content subjects with English as a second language. Linguistic minority students learn English and use it as a vehicle for learning other academic subjects. Which type of ESL program model best fits this description?

a. The model of pull-out programs for ESLs
b. The model of two-way language immersion
c. The model of content-based ESL programs
d. The model of sheltered English instruction

44. A teacher is creating a rubric to assess students' presentations on explorers around the world. She has broken up the scoring into several categories related to both language objectives and the standards for social studies. Which category does NOT relate to language assessment?

a. Content
b. Organization
c. Delivery
d. Fluency

45. To apply research findings about how English language learner (ELL) students' school performance is influenced by cultural factors, which of the following teacher practices is MOST appropriate?

a. Teachers respond to ELLs' culturally mediated learning approaches by modifying instruction.
b. Teachers respond to ELL students by emphasizing language instruction over cultural factors.
c. Teachers respond to ELLs by developing comprehensive curricula for US cultural immersion.
d. Teachers respond to cultural factors by grouping ELL students sharing cultural backgrounds.

46. In order to talk about science concepts in English, if ESL students have learned scientific _______ concepts in their native languages, they can transfer these to English.

a. pragmatic
b. semantic
c. discourse
d. syntactic

47. An elementary English language learner (ELL) student has learned some English expressions from American classmates and demonstrates his learning by greeting the school principal, "Hey, man! What's up?" This child has not yet mastered which feature of pragmatics?

a. Idiom
b. Setting
c. Register
d. Purpose

48. A high school English teacher wants to teach the importance of considering the audience in writing to her students. Which activity would promote this pragmatic feature?

a. Students watch their teacher model how to write a letter to her family, the principal, and to an author she admires, and then they compare these letters.
b. Students study different essays, such as persuasive and expository, and compare and contrast the different features of these texts.
c. Students discuss topics that would interest them in cooperative groups and write a joint poem to present to the class.
d. Students are asked to pretend to be news reporters for news organizations with different political stances and write articles showing those perspectives.

49. Students in a second-grade beginning-level English Language Development (ELD) class are performing actions while the teacher gives oral commands that are being modeled by the teacher such as "stand" and "jump." This is known as what type of strategy?

a. Total physical response
b. Direct teaching and mastery learning
c. Common underlying proficiency
d. Call and response

50. Which of the following assignments incorporates all four Cs of creativity, critical thinking, collaboration, and communication throughout the entire activity?

a. Having students independently plan and then execute their own projects to solve problems
b. Having students in small groups plan problem-solving projects and execute them independently
c. Having students in small groups plan and execute original problem-solving projects as a joint effort
d. Having students independently plan and then execute original problem-solving projects together

51. Regarding Krashen's Monitor hypothesis, which of the following personality traits is NOT associated with overusing learning as a monitor of L2 performance?

a. Introversion
b. Extroversion
c. Doubtfulness
d. Perfectionism

52. A brand-new English language learner from Guatemala has joined a teacher's English Language Development (ELD) class. Which of the following is not information that is important to gather about the student regarding language learning?

a. The student's first-language proficiency
b. The student's interests and dislikes
c. The student's previous language experience with English
d. The student's legal status for residency

53. Which of the following is accurate regarding social distance and psychological distance relative to English language learner (ELL) students?

a. Social distance refers to a student's degree of comfort with learning a second language.
b. Psychological distance is a student's degree of contact with a new language community.
c. Psychological distance influences include attitude, integration, and cultural congruence.
d. Social distance is influenced by dominance, enclosure, cohesiveness, residence length.

54. Which of the following is an example of nonmaterial cultural ?

a. Clothing that is worn in the culture
b. Food that is common in the culture
c. Language spoken within that culture
d. Patterns often used in the culture

55. The new ESL teacher is compiling a file of information for each of her students. Her files include level of L1 education and literacy; level of L2 competency in the four modalities of speaking, writing, listening, and reading; the type and depth of English study the student has undertaken; the student's interests and personality type; and the most effective learning styles for the particular student. What does the teacher most likely intend to use these files for?

a. She will use the information they contain to vary her lessons to meet each student's specific needs.
b. She will send them home periodically so that parents can read her notes and sign off on them.
c. She will use the information to separate the students into their respective levels in future classes.
d. She will share the students' files with classmates so they can get to know one another on a more intimate, personal level.

56. Two teachers are discussing one of their mutual students. The term "communicative competence" comes up. What aspect of the student's development are the teachers discussing?

a. Her willingness to listen to another speaker's message and respond kindly and appropriately
b. Her ability to use the elements of language (syntax, phonology, morphology, semantics) together with an understanding of social expectations and to use spoken messages that are appropriate in terms of how they are manifested and when, in the course of conversation, they are used
c. Communicative competence is transparently interchangeable with CALP; the teachers are discussing her social language skills.
d. Communicative competence is transparently interchangeable with BICS; the teachers are discussing her academic language skills.

57. A teacher wants to become more informed about how an individual English language learner (ELL) student's family applies native cultural traditions related to social occasions and interactions. If the teacher were to do only one of the following, which one would be MOST useful for this purpose?

a. Informal conversation with classmates
b. Interviews in this culture's community
c. Home visits with this student's family
d. Reading books on the family's culture

58. Communicative competence consists of grammatical, sociolinguistic, discourse, and strategic competence and is currently the objective of many language education programs. To whom can the spread of its ideas best be attributed?

a. Canale and Swain
b. Chomsky
c. Hull
d. Krashen

59. Which of the following perspectives or concepts can be characterized as exclusive rather than inclusive?

a. Cultural congruence
b. Cultural relativism
c. Cultural pluralism
d. Ethnocentrism

60. Which of the following English words has a Greek origin?

a. Calorie
b. Calendar
c. Calumny
d. Calisthenics

61. An 11th-grade government teacher has several advanced-level English learners in his class. He assigned an essay that must be written and typed at home. To write the essay, students must choose and conduct research online for one of the three branches of government. What should he consider when assigning this paper to his English learners?

a. Finding appropriate supports such as summary frames for their writing
b. Remembering not to assume that all of his students have access to technology at home
c. Letting his English learners choose a different topic so that they can discuss their own culture and government
d. Allowing his English learners to work on the essay during class while the other students complete a different activity

62. Of the following statements, which is accurate regarding front-loading vocabulary for English language learners (ELLs)?

a. Before assigning reading, teachers must first scan the text to identify problematic vocabulary.
b. For comprehension, students need a working knowledge of 75% of the vocabulary in the text.
c. Identifying their students' Lexile levels will not help teachers for front-loading text vocabulary.
d. Identifying student Lexile levels is useful, but Lexile Analyzer does not help with specific texts.

63. Which language function does the following scenario entail?

Teacher: "Take out your textbooks, and open to page 11."

a. Instrumental
b. Informative
c. Heuristic
d. Regulatory

64. An English Language Development (ELD) teacher noticed that when she had administered a listening test to her students twice, the scores were not reliable. What would indicate to her that the test is not reliable?

a. The scores were drastically different among all of the students.
b. The test took too long for students to complete the first and second time.
c. The test did not ask questions relevant to the topic that was being taught.
d. The scores were different the first and second time students took the test.

65. Among English language learners (ELLs), which students must deal with both a different alphabet and different directionality in English orthography?

a. Speakers of Slavic languages
b. Speakers of Romance languages
c. Speakers of Semitic languages
d. Speakers of Germanic languages

66. A student from a culture with a rich oral tradition is having difficulty starting an assignment to write an essay describing an experience. How could the teacher help by contextualizing the assignment to help access prior student knowledge?

a. Give the student a list of key descriptive vocabulary translated from L1 to L2.
b. Instruct the student to write the essay in L1 first and then translate it into L2.
c. Give the student a recorder, tell him or her to dictate a story, and then write it.
d. Instruct the student to use an earlier native language composition as a guide.

Refer to the following for question 67:

An advanced placement physics teacher has several advanced-level English learners in her class. She is required to use a textbook assigned by the district based on what has been formally adopted by their state department of education. She gives a variety of tests including those that are provided by the textbook publisher.

67. She can best address the English learners' needs relative to textbooks in content-area classes with which of the following?

a. Give ELL students textbooks issued for lower grade levels in the subject.
b. Give ELL students condensed or summarized booklets as substitutes for the textbook.
c. Give ELL students the same textbook and provide L1 translations of key terms as needed.
d. Give ELL students visual graphic organizers and manipulative objects instead of the textbook.

68. An Iranian English language learner (ELL) student relocated to Atlanta, Georgia, is trying to relate an enjoyable recent tourism experience to a classmate. Groping for the name of the place, he says, "Plantation." The classmate, assuming he visited an area antebellum plantation preserved as an historical attraction, responds, "You mean Stately Oaks in Jonesboro?" The ELL student replies, "No, it was . . . so beautiful, all the stars!" Instantly the classmate understands: "Oh, you mean the planetarium!" The ELL student confirms, "Yes! Planetarium!" (There are four planetaria in Iran, whereas many more US cities have them.) In correcting his own word substitution and the classmate's misunderstanding, which cognitive strategy did the ELL student use?

a. Repetition
b. Elaboration
c. Code-switching
d. Self-monitoring

69. For Grade 8 early to intermediate English language learner (ELL) students, which classroom activity would give them the best opportunities to receive comprehensible English input and produce comprehensible English output in purposeful, meaningful contexts?

a. The teacher introduces a new grammatical construction, gives explanation and examples to students, and has them paraphrase it and then find incorrect examples in brief text portions.
b. The teacher plays a video on a social studies topic, summarizes the video orally, and assigns students to write down new vocabulary words from the video in personal dictionaries.
c. The teacher has students read explanations of the phonological production of certain English sounds, plays them a recording of those phonemes, and has students practice them.
d. The teacher demonstrates a simple chemistry experiment, assigns students to pairs to try it themselves, and then assigns them to small groups to discuss their experiences.

70. When experts advise teachers to use cooperative learning techniques with ESL students, this relates most to which of the TESOL standards?

a. To use English for academic achievement in all subjects
b. To use English that is socially and culturally appropriate
c. To use English to get what the student wants
d. To use English for communication within social settings

71. Teachers of academic subjects in a school attend a training wherein an ESL teacher informs them of techniques for simplifying the English language they use to communicate with ESL students. Which of these principles is most reinforced for the teachers attending the training?

a. The collaboration of mainstream classroom and ESL teachers
b. The promotion of parental participation in student education
c. The incorporation of community resources in ESL classrooms
d. The application of ESL strategies within the classroom context

Refer to the following for question 72:

> Yin is an 11th-grade English learner from China. He has been taught at home to not speak to adults unless first spoken to. At first, his science teacher believes that he is too passive in class because he does not volunteer to answer in class; however, since he is also aware that sometimes silence in Yin's culture can mean respect rather than regret or embarrassment, he decides not to call on him in class.

72. What is the teacher's initial misunderstanding a result of?

a. The teacher holds incorrect stereotypes against Chinese students.
b. A cultural miscommunication is occurring due to a difference in cultures.
c. Yin has not yet assimilated to the minority culture.
d. Cultural pluralism is affecting the cultures that are a part of America.

73. Many times, ESL teachers must simplify a text so that students will be able to understand the ideas. Why is it important that the language be simplified by substituting common words for more abstract ones, by shortening sentences or turning a long sentence into two or three simple ones, or by deleting unnecessary information while modifying the concepts and ideas as little as possible?

a. ESL students generally are not at the same grade level as their English-speaking peers; therefore, they cannot understand texts that are too difficult.
b. Grade level content is essential. Simplifying language without simplifying content will help ESL students remain at grade level.
c. The statement is incorrect. It is essential to modify both language and ideas by stripping them of detail, clarifying language, and making ideas as simple as possible.
d. It's important to simplify texts by reducing and eliminating content to make it more understandable and, at the same time, retaining as much of the original language as possible. This is to challenge LEPs to reach the highest linguistic goal they can achieve; if language is stripped of meaning, it is more transparent and carries less cultural weight.

74. If a student is identified with both English language learner (ELL) status and visual impairment, which of the following classroom interventions or modifications will NOT address the student's needs best?

a. Differentiating instruction for the language level
b. Preferential seating at the front of the classroom
c. Magnifiers, large-print text, and audio recordings
d. More reading or written than heard or oral assignments

75. Which was NOT one of the impacts on English language learners of federal policy following the *Lau v. Nichols* US Supreme Court Case in 1974?

a. Schools must take steps to ensure adequate education for English language learners.
b. Schools are not allowed to assign English learners to vocational tracks instead of teaching them English.
c. Schools cannot deny children of illegal immigrants an education.
d. Schools cannot designate English learners into special education programs based on their English language skills.

76. Which law requires all US state educational agencies "to take appropriate action to overcome language barriers that impede equal participation by students in an instructional program"?

a. The ruling in the *Lau v. Nichols* (1974) case
b. The decision in *Castañeda v. Pickard* (1981)
c. The Equal Education Opportunity Act (1974)
d. The decision in the *Plyler v. Doe* (1982) case

77. Which of the following is the best example of giving ESL students appropriate feedback in response to their developing English-language skills?

a. Correcting every single mistake every time a student makes one
b. Pointing out serious errors after the class has finished an activity
c. Disregarding student errors in planning additional class practicing
d. Accepting good work via silence while highlighting only mistakes

78. Which of the following is a strategy important to use in Specially Designed Academic Instruction in English (SDAIE) lessons?

a. Hands-on activities
b. Guarded vocabulary
c. Cooperative learning
d. All of these

79. Some refugee English language learner (ELL) students lack prior formal education and print literacy skills, yet they have excellent storytelling skills, which American educators are able to use to inform their instruction in English language writing. This teaching approach, based on the assumption or view that developmental pre-reading and prewriting skills can be taught, is associated MOST with which of these underlying theories?

a. The emergent literacy theory
b. The interactive reading theory
c. The funds of knowledge theory
d. None of these

80. Which type of theory most attributes language acquisition to the influences of context, world knowledge, and motivation to achieve goals?

a. Social interactionist theory
b. Behaviorist theory
c. Cognitive theory
d. Nativist theory

81. A teacher has given a class of English language learner (ELL) students some sample essay texts to analyze. They analyze and discuss whether each essay organizes its ideas well and produces a sense of unity through using a thesis statement and topic sentences throughout. What is the teacher instructing the students in?

a. Cohesion
b. Coherence
c. Both of these
d. Neither of these

82. When the middle schools receive the test results later on, they see that the students' scores are reported in both raw and scaled form. The scaled scores will be most useful for:

a. Determining exactly how many questions students got right and wrong
b. Determining which types of questions students had the most trouble with
c. Comparing students' performance across different administrations of the same test
d. Predicting students' performance in the classroom and on future tests

83. When teachers assess student performance using continua, which of the following is considered a disadvantage?

a. More precise evaluative descriptions of student performance instead of discrete grades
b. Greater difficulty in comparing student, class, and school scores without exact numbers
c. Performance ranges are more realistic and accurate than exact numbers or cutoff scores
d. Greater compatibility with individualized student assessment than standardized testing

84. A middle school English Language Development (ELD) teacher is teaching English learners Greek and Latin roots. What skill is this teacher developing?

a. Phonics
b. Syntax
c. Semantics
d. Morphemes

85. According to federal law, which is true of Title III grants?

a. These grants do not support the initial development of ESL programs.
b. These grants may be decreased and/or eliminated from ESL programs.
c. These grants must not be used for capacity building with ESL programs.
d. These grants can be depended on in perpetuity to fund ESL programs.

86. A sixth-grade math teacher considers several tools and strategies to use with her beginner-level English learners that would support their vocabulary development in math. She is specifically teaching surface area. Which tool would best serve this purpose?

a. A calculator so that they will not have to worry about making calculation errors
b. Worksheets with surface area practice problems
c. A page with pictures of three-dimensional objects and key terms that relate to these objects
d. A chart of essential formulas that they can use during tests and homework

87. A seventh-grade math teacher considers how to use scaffolding to support her students in learning how to create a graph using a table. What is the first step she should take in scaffolding?

a. The teacher completes the task with student input.
b. The teacher models how to complete the task to students.
c. Both the teacher and student share the task duties.
d. Students try to complete the task on their own without support.

88. A ninth-grade early-intermediate level English learner has a low threshold for failure and often stops trying when a task is difficult. What could be a strategy the teacher uses to support this learner?

a. Give the student easy tasks so he is successful.
b. Allow the student to have some choice, and slowly increase the difficulty of the activities.
c. Speak with the student's parents so that they can consider moving the student to a different track that will move through concepts more slowly.
d. Pair the student so that he does work only with another student.

89. An elementary school teacher expecting a new English language learner (ELL) student has read that people from this student's culture are often embarrassed by being praised in front of a group, so he plans to use stickers showing approval on the student's written assignments. Which step should precede this strategy?

a. Explaining to the student's parents the rationale for this strategy
b. Doing extra reading about characteristics of the student's culture
c. Asking coworkers about alternatives for positive reinforcement
d. Finding out whether this individual student has that cultural trait

90. What are the characteristics of an additive educational program?

a. It works with students who come from families with a history of drug or alcohol abuse. By starting therapy at a young age, the hope is that these children won't grow up to become addicts as well.
b. It is a social studies program that primarily focuses on the positive. It means that only those characteristics of a social group that are joyful, exuberant, or peace-loving will be taught.
c. It is a program that uses a student's culture of origin as a scaffold to teach her about her new culture.
d. It is a program that explores all the ways advertisements exploit cultures by furthering stereotypes and prejudices.

91. When assessing the language abilities of an ELL child, which of the following would be considered significant, consistent exposure to English?

a. Three or more days weekly of an English-language school, day care, or babysitter
b. Being exposed to the English language incidentally from the television
c. Exposure to the English language at different times in the community
d. Having been exposed to English language that is spoken at home

92. The parents of a first-grade LEP student do not want her placed in a special education classroom; they feel that she is better off in a regular classroom at her grade level. The classroom teacher, ESL teacher, school counselor, and diagnostician are all certain that she has several interrelated learning disabilities, as well as some emotional issues. Given that she is unlikely to thrive in a regular classroom, will cause an extra burden of work to the teacher, and will without doubt be disruptive and cause problems for other students, can she be placed in special education classes?

a. No; parental permission is required.
b. Yes; parental permission is required, but in its absence a building can, with requests from four or more professionals, be overridden.
c. Possibly; the school must refer the case to Children's Protective Services, which will make the final decision.
d. Temporarily, while the district takes the parents to court to force the issue. If the court rules in favor of the parents, the district must place the student in a regular classroom, pay the parents' legal costs, and pay a fine if the judge so orders. If the court rules in favor of the district, the parents must pay all court costs, but no fine can be assigned.

93. Among informal assessments of English language development (ELD) of English language learner (ELL) students with low literacy, which of the following formats typically would best enable them to demonstrate their English language knowledge?

a. Listening to spoken teacher questions and responding by choosing among pictures
b. Reading written teacher questions and responding by writing down their answers
c. Listening to spoken teacher questions and responding by writing their answers
d. Reading written teacher questions and responding by choosing from pictures

94. Which of these MOST accurately differentiates characteristics of prejudice versus discrimination?

a. Prejudice involves uninformed opinions, while discrimination involves unfair treatment.
b. Prejudice involves the actions one takes, while discrimination involves what one thinks.
c. Prejudice involves judging ahead of time, while discrimination involves fine distinctions.
d. Prejudice involves exactly the same things that discrimination involves; they are equal.

95. The faculty members in an elementary school's ESL program make a practice of inviting their students' families to participate in making decisions about school programs and in other school projects and activities. What is their most likely reason for doing these things?

a. They know parents teach children specific language aspects better if informed on instruction.
b. They know English language development is affected by families' positive attitudes to school.
c. They know families model purposeful communication better if participating in school activity.
d. They know curricular familiarity helps families evaluate effectiveness of language instruction.

96. Sylvia is a high school English language learner (ELL). When given oral discourse activities, she is very good at addressing points classmates have just brought up, organizing her ideas, unifying her overall message, and finding appropriate English words and phrases to make connections and transitions between sentences; however, she speaks very slowly, with many pauses and interruptions between phrases and sentences. On which area does she need to work?

a. Responsiveness
b. Coherence
c. Cohesion
d. Fluency

97. Which of the following is not a component of using Specially Designed Academic Instruction in English (SDAIE) to design a lesson for English learners?

a. Teacher attitude
b. Comprehensibility
c. Interaction
d. Structured English Immersion (SEI)

98. A Mexican student is aghast when an American classmate tries to communicate with her in Spanish and translates *embarrassed* to *embarazada.* The teacher helps her explain to the American classmate that, in Spanish, this word means pregnant. What is this difference an example of?

a. Cognates
b. False cognates
c. Multiple meanings
d. A syntactic mistake

99. Which activity is likely to be MOST effective in helping elementary school English learners develop familiarity with the concept of print?

a. Define the concept of print to students, and write the definition on the board.
b. Read aloud a book to learners while pointing at the words being read.
c. Encourage discussions in the students' first language, and translate into English.
d. Begin silent reading activities so students develop a love for reading.

100. If a teacher assesses advanced-level English language learner (ELL) high school students' writing tasks using holistic scoring, which of the following is a limitation of this method?

a. Scoring procedures are complicated.
b. Students do not get explicit feedback.
c. The method is more time-consuming.
d. The grades are largely useless as they cannot track progress.

Answer Key and Explanations for Test #2

1. C: When planning Specially Designed Academic Instruction in English (SDAIE) lessons for English language learner (ELL) students in content-area subjects, teachers should find ways to integrate all language skills—listening, speaking, reading, and writing—into instruction across the curriculum. Therefore, the most effective use of SDAIE lessons would be to assign reading tasks, writing tasks, oral presentations as speaking tasks, and discussions as listening and speaking tasks, not only in English language development (ELD) classes but also in math, science, social studies, and other content subjects. Choices (A) and (B) do not integrate all four domains—listening, speaking, reading, and writing—across the curriculum but limit instruction to only two of those in one or two subjects. Choice (D) omits listening and speaking tasks entirely across the curriculum. Waiting for students to reach higher oral English language proficiency (ELP) levels is ineffective without providing instructional listening and speaking tasks to enable them to attain those levels.

2. C: Before World War II, there were no school system-wide initiatives to address the education of ESL students in America. There were no ESL programs then, not even in large city school systems (A). There were, however, no laws to prohibit non-English-speaking students from enrolling in American schools (B). Statistically, no more ESL students with low English language proficiency (LEP) attended bilingual parochial schools (D) than public schools.

3. C: Rosetta Stone, a popular language-learning system, has a website with interactive software including live lessons online, community-building activities, games, and more designed to teach learners how to speak foreign languages including English with native-like proficiency. The English as a second language (ESL) Jobs Forum (A) is a website for teachers of ESL to obtain information about training, teacher certification, job openings, and teaching. The Reading Plus system (B) is a web-based program designed to help students in Grade 3 and higher to improve not English speaking but reading proficiency including vocabulary, comprehension, silent reading, fluency, and standardized test scores. Easy Writer, from Software for Students (D), is a software application that uses authentic writing tasks to help English language learners (ELLs) develop their English writing, not speaking, proficiency.

4. B: The first step in writing workshops is prewriting. This includes activities such as brainstorming through the use of mind maps or graphic organizers. In addition, prewriting could include discussing ideas, reading texts, and creating role-playing activities. In prewriting, students are not yet crafting their texts, so sentence stems and word banks should come later in the writing workshop process. This means that Answers A and C are not the first step.

5. B: Changing the teacher's level of physical contact based on the student's perceived comfort levels and cultural norms would not be wise for the teacher to do so because it can be construed as favoring certain students over others. Furthermore, it can confuse students as to what the norm is around physical contact between a figure of authority such as the teacher and the student. Maintaining clear and consistent expectations and behaviors helps students learn what the norm is for the school's culture.

6. B: Incorporate extra-linguistic materials into instruction, such as realia, gestures, and enactments. Comprehensibility will be increased by direct, hands-on involvement and clues to meaning that exist in the physical context of the classroom.

7. D: Assimilation is the process in which an individual tries to adopt the culture of the dominant culture and rejects his or her culture. Accommodation is a process in which members of the mainstream culture and the minority culture both learn to adapt to one another. Biculturalism is when an individual is able to function in two different cultures. Culture shock occurs once the initial excitement of being in a new culture wears off and the individual feels frustrated by the confusion and differences between the two cultures.

8. C: This is an example of the ESL teacher's participation on the schools Language Proficiency Assessment Committee (LPAC). Contributions to (A) are contributions to the Admissions, Review and Dismissal (ARD) meeting. In the example they are trying to assess language proficiency, not decide about admitting, reviewing the progress of, or dismissing a student. Serving on (B) is serving on the Site-Based Decision Making (SBDM) committee, which refers to making decisions for a particular school location rather than assessing a student's language proficiency. An example of serving as a resource for other teachers (D) would be sharing ESL information with them to help them teach mainstream subjects to ELL students, rather than assessing a student's language proficiency for placement purposes.

9. D: They do not accurately reflect native speakers' proficiency and therefore cannot accurately reflect non-native speakers' proficiency. A study examined the efficacy of the Language Assessment Scales-Oral, the Woodcock-Muñoz Language Survey, and the IDEA Proficiency Test by giving all three to both native English-speaking non-Hispanic Caucasian and Hispanic students from all socioeconomic levels. Interestingly, these L1 English speakers did not receive similar results from the three tests, which ostensibly assessed for the same information. In fact, none of the native English speakers who were given the Woodcock-Muñoz Language Survey were assigned fluent status. On the other hand, all students scored as fluent in the Language Assessment Scales-Oral, while 87% were described by IDEA Proficiency Test results as being fluent. L1 English speakers who do not uniformly score in the fluent range throw into doubt the assessment's ability to accurately reflect an L2's proficiency.

10. A: Affective factors include self-esteem, motivation, levels of anxiety, and teacher expectations. Cognitive factors include learning style and strategies, whereas political factors might include language policies both nationally and at the local level, school organization, and school policies and practices. Sociocultural factors include family expectations, acculturation levels, community effects, and family values. All of these factors play a role in a student's language development, but the one being described in the example relates to affective factors.

11. A: Giving English language learner (ELL) students a glossary of English chemistry terms to write experiment reports is an example of scaffolding a content-area assessment task. Choices B, C, and D are all examples of scaffolding English language development (ELD) assessment tasks for ELL students.

12. D: Community members are valuable resources for educators to involve in their schools and classrooms. They can contribute to student learning by sharing their insights about different cultural traditions; linguistic traditions, backgrounds, and information; and also the expertise in various content area subjects that they possess.

13. B: Studies find that, when students have had no prior formal education in their native languages, they take longer to develop academic language in the L2 they learn. For example, it can take them 7 to 10 years to develop academic language proficiency in the L2 instead of 5 to 7 years if they have had previous formal schooling in their L1s. However, lack of formal education does not interfere as much with developing basic social communication skills in the L2 (A) because (1) primarily, these are less demanding cognitively; (2) students are more constantly exposed to social language in their everyday lives; and (3) students develop these skills of necessity for everyday interactions. When students transfer features of their L1s to the L2, some features are incompatible and constitute negative transfer, (C) while others are compatible and constitute positive language transfer (D): Either or both can occur.

14. D: Although each of these answers can be correct, think-alouds are most often used to promote reading comprehension through modeling what a good reader does while reading. Many students benefit from being explicitly taught how readers engage with the text rather than absorb passively, as is shown in Answer D. Students may learn vocabulary or sentence structures, which are represented in Answers A and B, but think-alouds are used as a metacognitive strategy. Using new vocabulary words can help build students' language knowledge but does not necessarily relate to think-alouds. Furthermore, although this strategy does work on listening comprehension, the main purpose is to develop strategies around reading comprehension. To further support students, the teacher can write down what he or she has said to aid with visual support.

15. C: According to experts, one guideline for multicultural instruction is for educators to share autobiographical information relevant to their class content. For example, if a teacher has visited some students' native countries, sharing this information can make students feel more at ease with the teacher, which can improve their class performance. Educators should share such experience not only in general terms but also in ways pertinent to the class. Experts say that educators should also establish contexts in their classes wherein students are comfortable sharing their own personal perspectives. For example, a heterosexual teacher of a women's studies class that includes lesbian, gay, bisexual, and transgender (LGBT) issues could derive advantages through knowledge that some students who are openly lesbian, gay, bisexual, or transgender want to share their academic and personal perspectives on the content of the class.

16. A: For listening, assessing descriptions and narrations of technical and factual material is an example of the Advanced level of an integrated ESL rubric. For speaking (B), reading (C), and writing (D), the choices are examples of the Intermediate level of an integrated ESL rubric. Examples of the Advanced level for these include: Speaking—Designing and giving speeches on academic subjects, including references to outside research sources; Reading—Formulating opinions about complex academic papers and articles 1–10 pages long; and Writing—Composing expository essays that make references to outside research resources.

17. C: Schools can provide training to diverse parents in effectively tutoring their children at home in math, reading, and other school subjects. It is also appropriate and important for schools to offer parent education about specific disabilities, which can help parents detect these in their children, recognize need for referral, or become informed about school and other services available for students with disabilities and about how to work with disabilities if their children have them. Prenatal care information is another area that should not only be left to Planned Parenthood; schools also can offer parent training classes with this information, which is often much needed and appreciated. Another area where schools can help is with information on free or reduced-cost aftercare opportunities, which are not only available from community agencies.

18. A: Cultures differ in their level of cooperation and competitiveness. In particular, some indigenous cultures promote cooperation rather than competition. Although it is important not to generalize and instead gain a deeper understanding of the culture, this can offer the best explanation from the choices. Although the school may be strict, it does not mean that students will not embrace fun during school. Furthermore, most cultures have different games and aspects of play and entertainment.

19. D: Pacing, that is, slowing down or speeding up instruction, is probably the dimension most frequently applied in teaching strategies for differentiating instruction because it is effective, inexpensive, and simple. Differentiating instruction via varying complexity (A) is effective but demands more teacher preparation, skill, and appropriate learning materials to implement. For challenged students, it requires removing confusing elements, making lessons even more sequenced and organized, and focusing even more on major concepts. For advanced students, it requires enriching instruction, allowing students to work with cross-curricular connections or time periods or subjects usually not expected for their grade levels. Novelty (B) involves new, different learning materials, modalities, or methods requiring additional teacher or school resources. Depth (C) often involves advanced students studying the same content more thoroughly.

20. A: One advantage of writing anecdotal notes as an assessment tool is that teachers can collect information about student skills and behaviors outside of assessment activities as well as during them; this can help teachers realize valuable insights into student learning and behavior. The fact that such notes are not standardized unless the teacher incorporates norms or criteria for comparison (B) is a disadvantage. An advantage of anecdotal notes is that teachers *can* record observations of individual student behaviors, which standard test instruments, checklists, and most other tools do *not* allow (C). The fact that anecdotal notes often lack any supporting context (D) is a disadvantage.

21. Essay question graders commonly look for the following elements in a strong response: strong content knowledge, clear organization, and effective arguments or examples. Language and usage are not usually strictly graded, but they can make a big impact on the clarity of your ideas.

Please use the provided rubric to make sure your response meets these common criteria. Try to have a friend or family member grade your response for you or take a break after writing your response and return to grade it with fresh eyes.

Constructed Response Rubric

Domain	Description
Content Knowledge	• The response directly addresses every part of the prompt. • The response demonstrates independent knowledge of the topic. • The response discusses the topic at an appropriate depth.
Organization	• The response introduces the topic, usually with a thesis statement or by restating the prompt. • The response directly addresses the prompt by providing a clear and concise answer or solution. • The answer or solution is supported by logical arguments or evidence. • The response restates the main idea in the conclusion.
Arguments and Examples	• The response provides a reasonable answer to the prompt. • The answer is supported by strong reasoning or evidence. • The response develops ideas logically and connects ideas to one another. • The reasoning and evidence provided act to support a unified main idea.
Language and Usage	• The response demonstrates effective use of grammar and uses varied sentence structure throughout the response. • The response demonstrates correct use of spelling, punctuation, and capitalization. • The response demonstrates strong and varied use of vocabulary relevant to the topic and appropriate for the intended audience.

22. A: English language learners (ELLs) with intermediate English language proficiency (ELP) can be impeded seriously in learning subject content by unfamiliar, content-specific language structures and vocabulary, particularly equation and formula syntax and technical terminology in mathematics and science subjects. When planning Specially Designed Academic Instruction in English (SDAIE) for middle school ELLs at the intermediate level of ELP, the teacher can give them better access to algebra content by integrating language objectives for these specialized elements into every lesson. Restricting instruction to skills and concepts at lower developmental levels (B) is inappropriate, as these do not match the students' developmental levels, regardless of their ELP levels. Putting off advanced lessons until ELLs reach advanced receptive ELP (C) is both inappropriate and unrealistic, as this could take too long for them to learn algebra at the right time; plus, individual student ELPs progress at varying rates. Lesson planning to avoid language just because math uses it less than other subjects (D) is also inappropriate for teaching SDAIE, which should still incorporate English language while emphasizing content learning, as its name indicates.

23. C: An appropriate intercultural communication strategy is to find out which terms are acceptable and unacceptable to certain cultural groups and then to use the acceptable terms to describe them. If others use unacceptable terms to describe them, members of all cultural groups should say so and say what they want to be called. Rather than substituting Americanized names, which does not make newcomers feel welcome (A), it is important to learn the correct spelling, pronunciation, and sequence of the names that others want to be called and any applicable titles showing respect. Another strategy is to avoid applying generalizations about cultural groups to individuals from those groups (B). Rather than maintaining your usual interpersonal space (D), it is better to observe the space people from other cultures use when determining the appropriate distance. Standing too close to or far from people from other cultures can cause them great discomfort.

24. C: Cultural concepts about time differ across different countries and cultures. Some cultures such as the United States value strict organization around time as well as efficiency and speed. Intelligence is often associated with speed in the American context. Other cultures, however, may not value time in the same way. It is important for teachers to be aware of their own time values and work within the school structure to support the student. This means that they may not be able to completely change the schedule or force the student to speed up.

25. D: A teacher working with an ESL student who is at the preproduction stage should incorporate gesture, pictures, manipulatives, and other extra-verbal tools into her teaching. The preproduction, or silent/receptive, stage of language acquisition is the first stage in which a learner must break into unfamiliar language that offers no easy entry. Visual images, coupled with the appropriate name, gestures indicating type or quality of movement, and other extra-verbal tools, will allow learners to begin to piece together the meanings that their first words carry.

26. B: The teacher should group English language learner (ELL) and native English-speaking students heterogeneously to give ELL students authentic opportunities to use English to communicate regarding academic content with both native and non-native English speakers. They should not be grouped homogeneously (A) as this will restrict their academic English communication to being only with other non-native English speakers. In some cases, it may be reassuring and supportive to place at least two ELLs per heterogeneous group (C), but this is not always necessary and, in some classes, can be impossible depending on numbers of students. As heterogeneous grouping will give ELLs opportunities to communicate with both native and non-native English speakers and homogeneous grouping will not, it is incorrect that the grouping will make no difference (D).

27. A: Specificity in a testing instrument refers to how much of the time the test correctly identifies that a child tested does not have whatever developmental delay or disorder the test is designed to measure. How much of the time a test correctly identifies that a child tested does have the targeted delay or disorder (B) is sensitivity rather than specificity. Good tests should have both high specificity and high sensitivity. When tests identify more issues than really exist (C) or fewer than really exist (D), especially screening tests, these results are considered testing errors. These can emerge in spite of high sensitivity and specificity.

28. B: Because these students had months of conversational English experience before starting school, listening to audio recordings of books being read aloud as they read them will access their English listening skills to inform and support developing their English reading skills. Vocabulary lists with translations (A) will facilitate L1–L2 vocabulary transfer but not access their English listening skills. Side-by-side English and L1 translated text (C) will facilitate L1–L2 reading transfer but not use English listening skills for English reading. Paired reading assignments (D) would help only if their partners were native English-speaking students or English language learner (ELL) students with higher levels of English reading proficiency; however, pairing within this same group of students would not. None knows any more about written English, and in even trying to help each other with reading comprehension, they would be more likely to converse in their L1 than in English.

29. B: Differentiation is an essential part of teaching; however, teachers should consider socio-cultural factors that influence instruction. If teachers believe that English learners are capable of less simply because of their language abilities, teachers set up students for failure. This can manifest in seemingly helpful ways by assigning only easy homework questions to English learners. Instead, carefully constructing word problems, pre-teaching necessary vocabulary, and considering the cultural assumptions made in word problems would be a better approach. Cultural values such as family are an important factor to consider; nonetheless, making blanket assumptions about all English learners should be avoided. Students come from diverse backgrounds and may or may not all have the same values, even if they speak the same primary language.

30. C: Refer the student to the school counselor, who is trained to help in situations such as this. It is essential that the teacher not violate the child's trust by reading the journal or showing it to anyone else. Such a violation of trust at this time could be very damaging. While the teacher should certainly monitor the situation and give close attention to the student's moods and behavior, she should not delay bringing the situation to the attention of the counselor.

31. B: When the student cannot categorize (A) an irregular verb conjugation by finding other irregular verbs conjugated the same way, he may simply need to memorize it. He cannot generalize (C) about it if he cannot find other irregular verbs conjugated the same way. In this case, he is applying his own cognitive processes rather than thinking about them (D).

32. B: Prior knowledge impacts students' English language development. Without the appropriate schema and background knowledge, students may have difficulty learning. Although psychological factors or learning disabilities may be at play, this particular learner is already at a beginning-advanced level, and a learning disability should not be the first conclusion a teacher jumps to when considering reasons for student difficulty. Cultural factors may also impact a student's performance at times; however, in this particular scenario, the student is not speaking in front of peers or showing off knowledge in a public way.

33. C: There are a multitude of reasons that may be an explanation for why the parents are not involved. These might include different values around family involvement in education. Some cultures do not have heavy family involvement in schooling due to a number of reasons such as respect toward the teacher. Lack of involvement, however, should not be confused with cultural deprivation or disinterest in education. On the contrary, many families have reported that they are supportive of their children's education. Moreover, although parental education has an impact, it does not mean that they are illiterate, especially because the student is in second grade.

34. C: Discourse includes the way that people interact and use language. Whereas syntax and morphology look at the sentence and word level of language, discourse looks at language in a broader sense in texts as well as behaviors. In particular, discourse can focus on how speakers take turns or show behaviors around listening and using cues when interacting. Discourse is highly contextual and cultural. Language used in the classroom differs significantly from language used at a soccer game or on the playground.

35. A: The student is omitting plural endings on nouns because the student's native language does not use a separate sound or letter to indicate plurality. The teacher needs to work with the student on English language morphology, like *-s* as a plural ending. Phonology (B) would pertain to correctly identifying and articulating the pronunciation of English language sounds. Semantics (C) would pertain to identifying and using English words with the correct meanings. Syntax (D) would pertain to identifying and using English sentences with the correct structure and word order.

36. D: The teacher should use all of the above strategies. By consulting with mainstream teachers to determine what content the students will be learning in upcoming months, she can choose or modify appropriate and understandable texts. The ESL teacher should only teach the content that she feels confident with, and she should emphasize deeper understanding of limited content over a glancing familiarity with a wider range of content.

37. B: The purpose of formative assessments is to assess students partway through a unit to see which parts of the units the students have mastered, as well as which parts of the unit may need to be retaught. These learning checks give the teacher a chance to see how the class is doing and how each student is doing individually. Formative assessments can be given in a variety of manners, including quizzes, tickets out the door, short essays or paragraphs explaining what was learned, as well as multiple other methods.

38. A: Homophones. Homophones sound alike but are spelled differently and have different meanings. Synonyms share meaning, homographs share the same spelling, and homonyms are like homophones, that share the same sounds, but they also are spelled the same. An example of a homonym is "lie," which can refer to lying down or to untruth.

39. B: Realia (A) and manipulatives (C) are both concrete, hands-on objects and materials, which younger children can access and understand more easily. Kindergarten through Grade 1 students will have more difficulty comprehending concepts unless they are accompanied by concrete objects they can see, touch, and manipulate. Analogies (B), that is, comparing one concept to another, are too abstract for children at these ages, as they do not provide anything concrete to help them understand the abstract ideas involved.

40. B: The most appropriate teacher strategy for this student would be to select from multiple strategies according to which is best for each subject. For example, when the student's reading and writing English language proficiency (ELP) levels permit the student to perform up to his or her subject ability levels, written assessments could be used, but all written assessments (D) should not be used considering the student's writing ELP level is much lower than speaking and listening ELP levels. Authentic assessments should be an option when the student's ELP levels prevent performing fully in some subjects, but these should not be the only assessments used (A). The teacher should scaffold any assessment tasks as needed but not necessarily all (C) if the student does not need it in some subjects or with some forms of assessment.

41. A: In Stage 1—Desired Results of Backward Design, established goals, understandings of big ideas, and what students will know and be able to do are addressed. In Stage 2—Assessment Evidence (B), what kinds of performance tasks and criteria will be used to assess student performance of their understandings are addressed. In Stage 3—Learning Plan (C), what kinds of instruction and learning experiences will help students attain the learning outcomes desired are addressed. There is no Stage 4 (D) in Wiggins and McTighe's Backward Design model.

42. C: Positive language transfer occurs when a student's first-language skills can be used to support learning the second language. This often occurs when languages are similar in structure and vocabulary. For example, an Italian speaker will have an easier time learning Spanish than Japanese due to positive language transfer. Teachers can use positive language transfer not only for language structure and vocabulary but also for skills such as phonemic awareness, knowledge of the reading process, and comprehension strategies.

43. C: The description given fits the model of the content-based ESL program because these programs simultaneously integrate academic content subject instruction with instruction in English as a second language. It does not fit the model of pull-out ESL programs (A) because in these programs, small numbers of elementary-school students are pulled out of their mainstream classrooms to have exclusive instruction in English for a part of their school day. It does not fit the two-way immersion model (B) because in this program, native English-speaking students and students speaking another native language are integrated so both groups learn each other's native language and both attain biliteracy. It does not fit the sheltered English instruction model (D) because in this type of program, ESL students in mainstream classrooms receive instruction from teachers using techniques to help them learn English as well as academic subjects.

44. A: Content focuses on the particular information that is included in the standards for that particular subject. The other three domains—organization, delivery, and fluency—all relate to language-area skills. These include speaking skills such as clear pronunciation, accurate use of grammar, and vocabulary. It also includes pragmatic skills such as use of eye contact and appropriate nonverbal communication with the audience. Organization focuses on the coherence and flow of the information given, which can relate to discourse and semantics.

45. A: Research studies find many English language learner (ELL) students perform below their abilities academically. Investigators believe cultural disparities between school and home contribute to these achievement gaps. They recommend teachers address diverse learning approaches through culturally responsive instruction as a solution rather than concentrating on language at the expense of culture (B), attempting to change ELL students culturally through curricula (C), or homogeneously grouping ELL students according to their cultural backgrounds (D).

46. C: Concepts of scientific discourse enable students to discuss science in any language. Research finds that students can transfer these concepts from L1 to L2, L3, etc. Pragmatic focuses on the social use of language to attain needs and wants. Semantic relates to the meanings of words/word combinations. Syntactic relates to the sequences of words and structures of sentences.

47. C: This child has not yet mastered the pragmatics feature of register. As dictated by social distance and norms, the expressions he learned from classmates are appropriate for informal use with fellow students but inappropriate for the more formal address required with an adult authority figure. While the expressions in the example are idiomatic (A), the student has indeed mastered them. Setting (B) is not the issue, as idioms are often used in school with classmates, just not with the principal. Purpose (D) is not involved. The student's purpose was to demonstrate his learning of American expressions, which he did; he just used the wrong register, which incorporates these idioms, to address the principal.

48. A: Pragmatics deals with the impact of context on the meaning of language. Pragmatics is highly cultural as it requires a shared understanding among the people communicating. One aspect of pragmatics is considering the audience. A teacher can model this by showing how language changes depending on whomever is the recipient of the communication. This is best shown through comparing letters with different recipients.

49. A: Total physical response (TPR) stems from a branch of behavioral theory that connects physical action to language. When teachers use TPR, they model an action while saying the word. Direct teaching and mastery learning also stem from behavioral theory; however, these strategies use rigid steps in which teachers follow a scripted lesson. Open Court is an example of direct teaching and mastery learning. Common Underlying Proficiency (CUP) refers to the idea that the primary language and the second language have shared underlying knowledge that allows competence in the second language. CUP is not a teaching methodology but relates to theories of second-language acquisition. Call and response is a strategy that uses choral replies between the teacher and the class, but it does not include physical actions.

50. C: Having the projects be original incorporates creativity; having them solve some problem incorporates critical thinking; having students plan and execute the projects as a joint effort incorporates collaboration and communication. Choice (A) incorporates critical thinking but not the other three Cs. Choice (B) incorporates critical thinking, collaboration, and communication in the planning stage but not in the execution stage. Choice (D) incorporates creativity and critical thinking, but it does not incorporate collaboration and communication in the planning stage. Thus, only (C) incorporates all four Cs throughout the entire activity.

51. B: Krashen correlates the personality characteristics of introversion (A), doubtfulness (C), and perfectionism (D) with overusing the conscious learning system as a monitor of L2 performance, and extroversion (B) with underusing learning as the monitor to plan, correct, and edit L2 speech. Learners described as optimal users of the monitor use it appropriately, neither too much nor too little.

52. D: Factors such as the student's name, age, level of first language proficiency, as well as English language proficiency are essential for teachers to know. In addition, information such as interests and previous academic success is important. Although whether a student is documented or undocumented affects a student's life, the right to education in the United States is not contingent upon legal status.

53. D: Social distance, not psychological distance (B), refers to a student's degree of contact with a new language community. Psychological distance, not social distance (A), refers to a student's degree of comfort with learning a new language. Psychological distance is influenced by factors including student motivation, culture shock, language shock, and individual ego permeability. Social distance is influenced by factors including student attitude, integration patterns, and cultural congruence (C), as well as social dominance, enclosure, cohesiveness, size, and the student's expected length of residence (D).

54. C: Culture includes both material and nonmaterial aspects. Nonmaterial cultural aspects are those that are not visible, such as language, values, customs, perspectives, beliefs, nonverbal communication norms, gender roles, and ideas around social status. Clothing, food, and patterns are all examples of material culture.

55. A: She will use the information they contain to vary her lessons to meet each student's specific needs. Because all students are individuals with unique abilities, experiences, and personalities, the most effective teaching methods must allow for modifying lessons to specific, individual needs. Parents don't benefit from having these notes sent home to them. Separating the students into groups based on language levels would not be the likely intent of these files, as each student likely has differing needs and interests that would make similar groupings difficult. Finally, it would be unethical to share a student's files with their classmates.

56. B: The teachers are discussing her ability to use the elements of language (syntax, phonology, morphology, semantics) together with an understanding of social expectations and to use spoken messages that are appropriate in terms of how they are manifested and when, in the course of conversation, they are used.

57. C: If the teacher wants to know specifically how an individual student's family observes cultural traditions related to social occasions and interactions, home visits with the family (including the student) would allow the teacher both to observe their practices and to interview, ask questions, and converse with the family members about their customs. Informal conversation with the student could elicit the desired information, but conversing with the student's classmates (A) would not yield the same specific information and observations as visiting with the actual student and family and neither would interviewing other members of the culture's community (B). Reading books on the culture (D) would not inform the teacher of one family's specific practices as well as the family itself could.

58. A: Canale and Swain. This theory determines that communicative competence consists of both organizational competence (competence with grammar and discourse) and pragmatic competence (sociolinguistic and speech acts) and is currently the objective of many language education programs.

59. D: Ethnocentrism (D) is the perspective of being oriented exclusively toward one's own culture, perceiving everything in terms of that culture, and ignoring, rejecting, or judging other cultures in comparison to one's own. Cultural congruence (A) is the perspective of acknowledging and accommodating diverse cultural backgrounds in education, health care, and so on, by making these services culturally responsive and compatible. Hence, cultural congruence is inclusive. Cultural relativism (B) is the perspective that characteristics of particular elements of a culture, for example, language, are differentially determined by features of that culture. For example, linguist Benjamin Whorf hypothesized that geographical features of a certain environment influenced the lexicon of the people living there, citing as evidence that Eskimo languages had more words for snow than other languages. It encourages examining cultures based on their contexts; thus, cultural relativism is inclusive. Cultural pluralism (C) acknowledges multiple and diverse cultural traditions and influences and is also inclusive.

60. D: *Calisthenics* has the Greek root *kalos,* meaning beautiful, or *kallos,* meaning beauty. (*Calligraphy* and *kaleidoscope* are from the same root.) *Calorie* (A) comes from the Latin *calor,* meaning heat (*caldron* is from the same source). Calendar (B) is from the Latin *calare,* meaning to call (*class, claim, conciliate, council,* and *nomenclature* are as well). *Calumny* (C) derives from the Latin *calumnia,* meaning trickery or slander, from *calvi,* meaning to trick or deceive (*cavil* and *challenge* are also from this root).

61. B: It is important to consider whether or not students have access to technology not only with English learners but with all students. Not every student has internet access at home, nor do they all have computers or laptops. At the advanced level, students should not be using summary frames for writing. Furthermore, it is important to ensure that students are meeting the objectives and standards required. If the objective of the task is to learn about the branches of government, the teacher should ensure that all students including his English learners meet grade-level standards. If he is interested in including culture and students' backgrounds, he could create an additional activity for the entire class in which students compare different models of government that include those from where his students came. It is important to be mindful of separating English learners from the rest of the class.

62. A: To frontload vocabulary, that is, pre-teach English language learners (ELLs) the vocabulary words used in a text that they will need to know in order to understand it before they read it, the first thing teachers need to do is to scan the text to identify the vocabulary words most likely to cause problems for these students. Research has revealed that, to comprehend text, students need a working knowledge of 95%—that is, most—of its vocabulary, not just 75% (B), so front-loading can be crucial for ELLs. An enormous help for identifying problem words in advance is to obtain student Lexile reading levels (C), which will give teachers an indication of which vocabulary they are likely to know and not know. Lexile Analyzer also will help teachers select specific texts (D) by scanning texts and returning their readability levels.

63. D: There are several different language functions, or ways that language is used. Halliday (1978) identified seven different categories: instrumental, regulatory, informative, interactional, personal, heuristic, and imaginative. Instrumental language functions are focused on getting needs met such as asking to go to the bathroom. Informative language functions focus on communicating information such as explaining the difference between toads and frogs in a presentation. Heuristic language functions are focused on investigating and acquiring knowledge. This might include asking questions about a topic in class. Regulatory language functions are those that attempt to control behavior. This could include commands such as "Stop!"

64. D: A test is reliable when it offers a relatively stable measure of the test taker's skills. This means that if the test is taken twice by the same person, the scores between the two should be similar. When an assessment is valid, this means that it measures what it should be measuring. For example, a test on reading comprehension should include questions regarding aspects of the passage rather than writing or speaking skills. An invalid test is demonstrated in Answer C. A practical assessment means that it does not take too much time or resources to administer. Answer B may be describing a test that is impractical.

65. C: Russian, Ukrainian, Bulgarian, Serbian, and many other (but not all) Slavic languages use variations of the Cyrillic alphabet, descended from the Greek alphabet. Its letters differ from those of the English alphabet, but the directionality is left-to-right horizontal as in English. Romance languages use a very similar alphabet to the English alphabet and are left-to-right horizontal. Semitic languages like Hebrew and Arabic use different alphabets than English, plus a right-to-left horizontal directionality. English is a Germanic language.

66. C: The teacher can best help access prior knowledge to facilitate the assignment by having the student dictate a story orally using a provided recorder and then transcribing the dictation. The rich oral tradition of the student's culture facilitates storytelling, and as speaking English typically precedes writing English for most English language learners (ELLs), the student can more easily transcribe spoken English into written English. Giving written translations (A) overlooks the student's oral tradition by providing only written materials in both languages. Telling the student to write in L1 and then translate it into L2 (B) also disregards speech in favor of writing. Telling the student to use an earlier L1 composition as a guide (D) is less appropriate because, if the student's native culture has a strong oral tradition, the student may not have had formal instruction in written language and may not have an earlier composition in the L1. Even if he or she does, it may be no help as a guide as it is not in English and may otherwise be too different from the current assignment.

67. C: Of the choices offered, the best way to address English language learner (ELL) student needs when state-issued textbooks are provided for all students is to augment them with L1 translations. Giving ELLs subject-content texts issued for lower grade levels (A) is inappropriate: Though the language in these texts may be at a level more accessible to ELLs, they will not receive grade-level subject content. Condensing or summarizing texts (B) is a less acceptable way to modify textbooks as reducing English language reading at the expense of full text means ELLs will not get the same textbook content and features as other students. Replacing textbooks with visuals and objects (D) to avoid English language reading deprives ELLs of the practice they need to develop their English language reading skills for accessing subject content in English.

68. B: The English language learner (ELL) student used elaboration to correct his word substitution error and the classmate's resulting misunderstanding. Using only a few words, but focusing on the key word *stars*, he gave the classmate enough information, combined with the similar sounds of the two words and the classmate's familiarity with local tourist attractions, for the classmate to infer he meant *planetarium* rather than *plantation.* He did not use repetition (A); repeating the same incorrect word would not have helped the way that elaborating with different words did. He did not use code-switching (C); for example, he did not say the Farsi افلاک سرا کیهان نما، for *planetarium*. He did not use self-monitoring (D) by reviewing the word he used and correcting it; he gave the classmate more explanatory information (elaborated).

69. D: The chemistry experiment incorporates teacher demonstration, paired work, and small-group discussion, affording students many opportunities for receiving comprehensible input and producing comprehensible output in English in purposeful, meaningful contexts. Answer choice A involves English input and output and paraphrase but not in such purposeful, meaningful contexts. Answer choice B also lacks such purposeful, meaningful contexts and does not give students opportunities for producing comprehensible output that others can hear and respond to as answer choice D does. Answer choice C lacks comprehensible input and output in meaningful contexts.

70. D: The Teachers of English to Speakers of Other Languages (TESOL) standards are (1) to use English for communicating in social settings; (2) to use English for academic achievement in all content-area subjects; and (3) to use English in ways that are socially and culturally appropriate. Cooperative learning techniques are most related to the social use of English. Some examples of expert advice for using English to achieve academically include labeling everything in the classroom in English; providing advance organizers to students; and providing a variety of learning media. Some examples of expert advice for using English in socially and culturally appropriate ways include teaching which settings/situations require formal vs. informal language use; using multicultural literature in classrooms; and inviting students' families to share their cultures.

71. D: This training most reinforces the principle of applying ESL strategies within the mainstream classroom context. It does not reinforce collaboration among mainstream classroom and ESL teachers (A) because the training involves instruction by the ESL teacher in information that the mainstream teachers learn, rather than their working together equally on teaching and/or learning. It does not promote parental participation (B) or incorporate community resources (C) as no parents or community resources are described as being involved.

72. B: Cultures have differing forms of communicating both verbally and nonverbally. In some cultures, speaking loudly over one another is acceptable, whereas in others younger individuals do not speak unless spoken to. Stereotypes are preconceived beliefs about a particular group that overgeneralizes and is harmful. Although stereotypes do play a large role in the classroom and should be an area of reflection for teachers, it is not the cause of the misunderstanding. Assimilation is a rejection of one's home culture to accept the values and beliefs of the dominant culture, not the minority culture. Finally, cultural pluralism is the idea that many cultures exist within a society. This is not what is at play in this scenario.

73. B: Grade level content is essential. Simplifying language without simplifying content will help ESL students remain at grade level. Language is the vehicle for meaning. It matters less how a student arrives at a relatively full understanding of the intended meaning, as long as she arrives at it at roughly the same time as her peers.

74. D: An English language learner (ELL) student with visual impairment would benefit from more listening and oral assignments instead of more read and written work, not vice versa. Differentiated instruction appropriate to the student's language level (A) will address student ELL needs. Preferential front-of-room seating (B) will address the visual impairment; so will providing magnifiers, large-print text, and audio recordings (C).

75. C: *Lau v. Nichols* was a landmark case for English language learners. It required that English learners have access to an adequate education; however, it was not until *Plyler v. Doe* in 1982 that the US Supreme Court ruled that schools could not deny enrollment based on a child's immigration status. *Lau v. Nichols* and subsequent federal policy required that schools offer equal education to English language learners, meaning they should not be placed in vocational tracks as an alternative to learning English or placed in handicapped courses based on their language abilities. It also required that schools communicate with families in a language they understand.

76. C: The Equal Education Opportunity Act (1974) mandates that no state can deny equal educational opportunity "by the failure by an educational agency to take appropriate action to overcome language barriers that impede equal participation by students in an instructional program." This means US State educational agencies not only cannot actively deny equal education opportunities, but moreover cannot passively deny such opportunities through not actively overcoming limited English proficiency. *Lau v. Nichols* (A) requires school districts to prevent discrimination against ESL students for not speaking English/limited English proficiency. *Castañeda v. Pickard* (B) requires school districts to determine LEP students' equal access to their programs and program effectiveness via a three-pronged standard. *Plyler v. Doe* (D) prohibits schools from requiring proof of legal immigrant status; documenting such status; barring undocumented students; asking about immigration status, including of students and/or parents; unequally treating undocumented students for determining residency; and for program eligibility, requires asking parents only for voluntary information.

77. B: If a teacher corrects ESL students every single time they make any kind of mistake (A), many of them would feel so inhibited they would be afraid to say anything. Many grammatical errors do not significantly interfere with communication. While serious errors should be corrected, teachers do better to make notes of these and then point them out after a class activity is over rather than interrupting the activity's/discussion's flow. Teachers should also make use of student errors to inform themselves of further student learning needs when they plan additional practice for the class (C). Rather than only highlighting errors, teachers should equally acknowledge good work at expressing ideas in English with encouraging words (D) during oral activities, and with check marks or similar written feedback on written assignments.

78. D: Hands-on activities (A) give English language learner (ELL) students authentic contexts for students to learn subject-area content while also developing their English language skills. Guarded vocabulary (B) simplifies English language to enable ELL students to connect new subject content to their first languages and prior experiences. Cooperative learning (C) enhances two-way communication with peers for academic learning purposes.

79. A: Emergent literacy theory assumes that developmental pre-reading and prewriting skills and behaviors like phonological awareness, language, conceptual knowledge, and letter knowledge can be taught. Interactive literacy theory (B) assumes that readers utilize knowledge at word, syntactic, and all other levels, including word decoding and interpretive inferences and predictions; move reciprocally between parts and whole; and synthesize sensory and intellectual components in reading for comprehension. The funds of knowledge theory (C) assumes that a student's home or community cognitive and cultural resources can inform classroom learning. Because (A) is correct, (D) is incorrect.

80. A: Social interactionist theory proposes that context (the surrounding environment and language used by people in it; world knowledge; and goals, motivating children to use linguistic utterances to attain them) influence language development. As its name indicates, this theory emphasizes social interactions in language acquisition. Behaviorist theory (B) emphasizes the environment's evoking certain responses in the individual through antecedents (preceding stimuli) and consequences (ensuing stimuli) to make a behavioral response more likely to occur and recur. Behaviorism applies these principles to verbal behaviors among all observable behaviors. Cognitive theory (C), like Piaget's theory of cognitive development, is constructivist, proposing individuals actively construct their learning and realities through interacting with and acting upon their environments. Piaget related language development to cognitive stages, each with new abilities developing. Nativist theory (D), like Chomsky's, says that people have innate language acquisition devices (LADs) and universal grammar, enabling rapid language acquisition and generation of endless linguistic combinations.

81. B: Organizing and connecting ideas and unifying an essay overall through use of a thesis statement and topic sentences are elements of coherence. Cohesion (A) is more specific, involving how individual words and sentences are connected through elements like reference, pronouns, conjunctions, and repetition.

82. C: A scaled score is most useful for comparing students' performance across different administrations of the same test. (For example, comparing this year's sixth graders to last year's, or comparing the performance of students at different schools who took different versions of the same test.) Raw scores simply indicate the number of questions a student answered correctly (A), and can only be used to compare students' performance on that specific version of the assessment.

83. B: When teachers use performance continua for assessment, they can describe student performance evaluatively with more precision than when they assign separate grades (A), an advantage. However, for comparing assessment scores among students, classes, or schools, the lack of exact numbers on a continuum is a disadvantage (B). On the other hand, the performance ranges provided by continua are more realistic and accurate than assigning exact numerical scores or referring to cutoff scores (C), an advantage. Except for comparisons (B)—in which case standardized tests are better—the superiority of continua for individualized assessment (D) is an advantage.

84. D: Morphemes are the smallest units of language that have meaning. For example, "devalue" is made of the morphemes "de," which means opposite or not, and "value," which means something that is important or useful. These cannot be broken down further. Greek and Latin roots are morphemes that help all students understand the meaning of words as well as be able to infer the meanings of words they do not know.

85. B: Under current federal law (Title III of the Elementary and Secondary Education Act as amended), federal grants support schools and districts in developing ESL programs; however, this law also directs schools and districts to use their grants for building their capacity (C) to continue offering high-quality ESL programs "after federal assistance is reduced or eliminated." This means that schools and districts cannot depend on these federal grants indefinitely for funding their ESL programs (D).

86. C: Although many of these tools may support students' learning, the tool that would best support vocabulary development is a page with key terms. Formulas are important, but in developing language, students should have a clear understanding of math terms related to this unit, such as surface area, sphere, and rectangular prism. Visual aids can support students' vocabulary development.

87. B: When considering scaffolding, teachers should first begin with modeling the task that they would like students to be able to accomplish independently. Students observe how the teacher completes the task. The next step is to then have the teacher complete the task with student input, with the teacher primarily completing the task. After that, teachers release responsibility to the students with guided support. Finally, the teacher allows the students to complete the task independently.

88. B: It is important to support the learner by giving him options as well as slowly increasing his confidence and tolerance for failure. It would not serve the student to continue giving him only easier tasks as this will not allow the student to grow and develop his skills. Furthermore, instead of considering placing the student in a lower track, which could make the situation worse, the teacher should communicate with parents to consider strategies both at home and school to support the student and improve his tolerance for failure. Placing him with another student constantly may lead to lower self-confidence.

89. D: Rather than explaining his rationale to parents (A), which assumes he will use the strategy, the teacher should first confirm or rule out whether this individual student actually does have the cultural trait about which the teacher has read. This also takes precedence over simply continuing to do more reading about the student's culture (B): Written materials, though valuable, may not give the same insights into as many dimensions of the culture as getting information directly from real students, parents, and community members from that culture. While coworkers could provide ideas for alternative strategies (C), the teacher still needs to find out the individual student's personal preferences first.

90. C: It is a program that uses a student's culture of origin as a scaffold to teach her about her new culture. An Additive Educational Program is one that supports and celebrates bicultural identity and encourages acculturation, rather than assimilation.

91. A: Experts advise that, for the purposes of assessing an English language learner (ELL) child's language abilities, full-time or three or more days weekly of exposure to English through school, day care, or babysitters constitutes significant, consistent exposure to the English language. However, incidental exposure to the English language from the television (B) or infrequent exposure to English language in the community (C) are considered casual, infrequent, and not qualifying as significant or consistent. Limited or recent exposure to English spoken at home (D), without at least full-time or three or more days per week in an English-language environment, does not by itself qualify as significant or consistent exposure.

92. A: No; parental permission is required. Under no circumstances can a student be placed in a special education classroom without the permission of a parent or a legal guardian.

93. A: If students have low literacy, they will have trouble reading and writing. In these cases, they may comprehend speech more easily. These students are also likely to have difficulty writing, so choosing from pictures would allow these students to more effectively demonstrate their knowledge.

At lower literacy levels, second-language acquisition (like first-language acquisition) typically proceeds from receptive to expressive; that is, student listening and reading skills precede speaking and writing skills. Therefore, oral questions will be easier for them to comprehend than written questions, and responding will be easier by selecting the correct picture among several than by speaking or writing their answers. Spoken responses would be easier than written ones; picture selection is easier than spoken responses.

94. A: Prejudice involves forming opinions of groups or individuals without any knowledge about them; discrimination involves treating certain groups or individuals differently than others in an unfair way. Prejudice more often involves thoughts; discrimination more often involves actions, not vice versa (B). Judging ahead of time is a literal meaning of the roots of the word *prejudice*; discrimination involving fine distinctions is a valid but separate meaning of the word *discrimination* or *discriminating* (C), as in matters of aesthetic tastes or sensibilities not applying to cultural conflict or treatment of other people. Prejudice and discrimination are related but are not exactly the same (D).

95. B: The ESL faculty members know that positive attitudes toward school and learning in students' families will promote the students' developing English-language proficiency, so they enlist family participation in school program decision-making and other school activities. They do not do this to promote parental teaching of specific language aspects (A) because ESL parents often do not have sufficient English-language proficiency themselves to teach specific aspects of English. They do not do it to promote family modeling of purposeful communication (C) because ESL parents may not have sufficient ELP to model purposeful English communication. They do not do it for families to evaluate the effectiveness of the school's language instruction (D) because doing this is the responsibility of the school district.

96. D: Sylvia needs to work on her fluency in oral discourse. Fluency is speaking at an appropriate rate, smoothly, and without pauses or interruptions. Her responsiveness (A) is good: She addresses points classmates have just mentioned. Her coherence (B) is good: She organizes her ideas and unifies her overall message. Her cohesion (C) is good: She finds words and phrase to connect and transition between sentences.

97. D: Structured English Immersion (SEI) is a separate program from Specially Designed Academic Instruction in English (SDAIE). SEI focuses on teaching only in English along with strategies to increase comprehension. SDAIE, on the other hand, may include a student's primary language for support. There are several key components of SDAIE. Teacher attitude is one aspect of SDAIE. In particular, teachers should be open-minded and willing to reflect and learn. Comprehensibility and interaction are also both essential components of the SDAIE model. Comprehensibility means including strategies that enhance comprehension, and interaction means that students have opportunities to discuss the content and ask questions.

98. B: This is an example of false cognates. Cognates (A) are words in different languages with the same origin and meaning (for example, English *dictionary* and Spanish *diccionario*). False cognates sound similar and may have the same origin but have different meanings as in the example given. This is not an example of multiple meanings (C), as *embarazada* is not used in Spanish to mean *embarrassed*; the Spanish word for *embarrassed* is *avergonzado*. The only other word for *pregnant*, *preñado,* refers only to animals, not people. This is an issue of semantics (word meanings), not syntax (D) or sentence structure or word order.

99. B: Some students who do not have literacy skills in their first languages may not understand the concept of print. The concept of print includes that print has meaning, how to hold a book and turn pages, reading from left to right and top to bottom, understanding that there are letters and words with spaces that separate words, and so on. Reading aloud allows students to see this in action as modeled by the teacher.

100. B: Holistic scoring methods are less, not more, complicated (A) and take less, not more, time (C) to assess written compositions; these are not limitations but advantages of holistic scoring. A limitation of holistic scoring is that individual students do not receive explicit teacher feedback (B). These grades are still useful in tracking overall progress (D).